HARDPRESS.NET
HOME OF HARD-TO-FIND BOOKS

A Nile Journal
by Thomas Gold Appleton

Address:
HardPress
8345 NW 66TH ST #2561
MIAMI FL 33166-2626
USA
Email: info@hardpress.net

A NILE JOURNAL.

A GHAWAZEE.

Egypt - Description 1574
'I. C,

A NILE JOURNAL

BY

Sold

T. G. APPLETON

" But her choice sport was, in the hours of sleep,
To glide adown old Nilus, when he threads
Egypt and Ethiopia from the steep
Of utmost Axumé until he spreads,
Like a calm flock of silver-fleecèd sheep,
His waters on the plain,—and crested heads
Of cities and proud temples gleam amid,
And many a vapour-belted pyramid."

SHELLEY—" *Witch of Atlas.*"

ILLUSTRATED BY EUGENE BENSON

Boston

ROBERTS BROTHERS

1876

Printed by R. & R. CLARK, *Edinburgh.*

ALICE, EDITH, AND ANNE.

MY DEAR NIECES,

THIS is a Journal I kept on the Nile for your entertainment and my own. It is like a thousand other journals, full of trivial details, and without learning or eloquence. Every year a little deposit of useful mud is left by the Nile upon its banks, and every year sees deposited upon counters of the London booksellers the turbid overflow of journalizing travel. Alas! it mostly has not the usefulness of the leavings of the sacred river.

We who so often have shared the pleasures of sailing on salt water, I trust may thus enjoy together a fresh water cruise on this most venerable of rivers.

T. G. A.

BOSTON, MASS.,
    Nov. 10, 1875.

LIST OF ILLUSTRATIONS.

A NILE JOURNAL.

Part First.

Monday, Nov. 30th, 1874.

WE are now fairly on the Nile. Our dahabeah, the *Rachel*, goes at a slapping pace before a wind which would be called lively in Boston Bay, and under a grey sky which might belong to the same latitude. We are alert and active for the first time, and this Journal gets launched out of the embayed sweetness of our lazier hours.

How unlike last evening when Egypt melted our being in its twilight, and we hung like flies in amber in the golden peace around us! Then the sky indeed died dolphin-like, passing through shades of tint which no other land knows, each more beautiful than the last; till the last picture, when night mixed with day held the beauty of both in solution, and that

B

seemed the fairest of all. The dying fire of Ammun Ré, the justified sun-god of old time, glowed carbuncle-like in sombre richness against the dark bars of the palms.

Such is our excuse for not beginning till now our contemplated Journal. To shoot the moment as it flies, to reproduce the seal of an impression as it stamps itself, to not be afraid of saying the truth, whether the meanest or most lofty, will be the aim of our pages. So many books have dribbled through our brains, written on the Nile, that their droppings must surely stain our paper, whether we would or no. But the oldest truth becomes new when freshly felt, and one may be obliged sometimes to tread in the footprints of a goose if only it has preceded us. A bread seal will hold the impression which has been cut in adamant. Let our minds only try to receive the true push of the object before them, and the bread seal shares in the majesty of what it reproduces.

We have only been a week willing

prisoners in our dahabeah, willing travellers of that river whose caravans stretch to earth's day dawn, and of that week only half the hours have been hours of progress.

Oh that embargo under the French bridge at Cairo! when motion seemed forbidden for ever, and we, chained to the bank, wearied of delay. How the friendly flies of Cairo said: "Here is our last chance! hit him in the eye once more before he leaves!" How the cheap sensuality of the table, so artistic and so bountiful that we feared to see the exhaustion of our stores before we were afloat, was a poor substitute for that superb sensuality of the soul which we hoped to feel farther on!

And yet we managed to get comfortable and happy before we began to sail. After familiarising our eyes with the *Rachel's* slender figure we got to love her; we saw that her lines were graceful, and promised the speed of which we had heard so much. She was bright, buoyant, beautiful, and clean within and without; and her bath, into which all Nile flowed, will wash from us the rust of narrow quarters. On her comely little deck we can breathe an air and give to our eyes a view as boundless as the desires of any mind, and which makes to us our dahabeah a universe. And we fished, as prisoners do, and caught the descendants of Memnonian fishes, from whose brains and through whose gills still flowed the silence of the centuries. We caught a few, but mostly did not. We had the nibble that enlarges in the mind as the victim recedes from the hook, and we liked to listen to the accurate Ruskallah's narration of his capture of a fish of sixty pounds weight, which fed the crew for three days, on a previous voyage. Of course it was a previous voyage. What fishes have we not caught—what wonders not seen—what achievements not done—all of us on that previous voyage! It is the catch-all of hope, and saves the disgrace of the present. But we did catch some, and eat them, and found they were belied.

They did not seem the muddy, worthless things which travellers describe, so let us hope the meaner things of our Nile journey may rise in our estimation, nor yet the grandest descend from their sublimer promise.

We looked with interest at the fellow-creatures Fate had given us for companions. We knew they would be part of our life—that the good or ill in them would modify our enjoyment, so that we glanced at them, trying to study their characters. Yet how vague, evanescent, uncertain, was the impression we received! We were trying to read a language whose alphabet we did not know. These Arab sailors moved about us, touched us—they were shadows still. Pleasantly spectral was their unknown smile, and the fire of hate or love in their eyes had been warmed at another sun than ours. When suddenly in their midst, we saw a head which had, somehow, the brand of Europe on it, which separated itself

from the others. It was our cook, Antonio, a Maltese, and whose relation to us
was to become every moment more affec-
tionate and intimate. If not our bosom
friend, he was to be lord supreme of that
neighbouring temple which such artists
make holy with their ministrations. And
a true artist he was! He could strike
a melody out of chickens or turkey poults
which showed that his soul felt the har-
monies of things, and his sauces would
accent the flavour of the dish he presented,
as a clever girl will wear a ribbon to bring
out the violet in her eyes. After he had
made our fancy dance with rahatlicum which
opened for us seraglios, or dates stuffed
with almonds which swept us to Badoura
and Bagdad, he would give us home
touches which brought the tears of grateful remembrance to our eyes. How his
fish balls reminded us of a past, starry with
fish balls! and brought to us again the
twang of New England in the tang of its
saltiness!   I write of our cook with

gratitude thus early, for he was the first we learnt to love. It was all we had then.

After a walk under the nigh palms, or perhaps a flying inspection of the fascinating aquarium of an unknown Pasha, we would divide the hours in our dahabeah between meals and sleep. Thus two days we loitered, when at last Achmed, king of men, our reis, appeared. He was a family man, and coming from Alexandria had thought it right to give his family the few hours he had to spare. He was a man lovely to look upon; as tall and flexile as a palm, brown as a date, and sweet with the same infused sunshine which makes that fruit so delightful. Nothing can disturb this tropical placidity. The *Rachel* being owned by the young men of Messrs. Tod and Rathbone, refused to pay her tax for the bridge at Cairo, claiming to be English. There were threats consequently of arresting the reis, but he came on board tranquil, and superior to all such disturbance.

Our equipage consists of twelve sailors, a reis and second reis, a cook and under cook, and a suffragee or waiter. This last, named Paolo, is a short, alert, active hand, who glides about our small cabin with the grace and dexterity of Kiki, our kitten. Our dahabeah is a small one, though there are many smaller. Cramped and limited as it is in accommodation, its sailing qualities and beauty fairly compensate for this.

We have a consort, the *Clara*, taking an English family, whose acquaintance we made at Shepheard's, up the Nile. She is twice as large as we are, and with her huge sail and long whip-like streamer seems master of the river. We all here fly our national flags, and in addition to these the *Rachel* flies at her peak the hollow diamond, and the *Clara* the Maltese cross. Yet, in spite of her grand looks, the *Rachel* beats her almost out of sight every day. When we start together in the morning, by sunset she is often three hours behind us ; but at night we crony and

OUR HELMSMAN.

nestle together. We combine for dusky evening walks with a fair English girl, between two Arabs holding enormous lanterns, or share with Mr. Porcher in sporting walks. We pay visits, ceremonious and other, and are really unhappy when long out of each other's company. The pleasure of this companionship in a strange land is easily imagined. The pilgrimage of these English figures across the plain, parasols and umbrellas well up, forcibly reminds us how far we are from the desolation and darkness of London. And behind an army of friends is following us. There, in the van, is the hero of Antietam with his fair wife, his monkey and his Philadelphia suite in an accompanying dahabeah; and there is Arthur of many dramas, and his dear mother, who bravely resolved at the last moment to venture towards the Equator. It gives me a pang to say that their boat is called the *Alice*, which name, in Arabic, even now floats from the reed-like yard. And then there are the Adamses of New York; and, for all I know, half-a-dozen other American boats, whose owners may have mustered at Shepheard's since we left.

As yet we have but once met the American flag; apparently it was on a native boat, but on somewhat roughly hailing it, we were told it was the property of the Arab-Amercian consul of Assouan.

So then, at last, we were off; the placid reis moving his hands with most graceful gestures, and the willing crew pulling at unintelligible ropes, which they sometimes do while calmly seated on the deck. At first they rowed us with their long red oars, lifted and depressed to a chant which gave them unity and time. I instantly saw a thousand Roman galleys with their oars flashing in the sunshine,—the barge of Cleopatra,—the grain-ship of Saint Paul,—and the many lateen sails that still hover along the shore of the Mediterranean. Our boat, though a river one, is legitimately de-

rived from the vessels of the olden day. Its
high poop and long cabin, in construction
the same as every other boat on the river,
must have been the fashion here since
Pharaoh. It is, of course, without a keel,
and bulges a little at its forefoot to catch
the mud-banks, and be the easier pushed
off. There are no reefs in its sails, but a
man sits always with the sheet in his hand
to let the sail fly if struck by a squall.
It has little or no bulwarks; the men
sleep on deck wrapped in their burnoos,
nearly on a level with the water; but we,
the gentry, sit towering above them on our
pretty deck, whose divans are deliciously
comfortable, and with a table in its midst
on which always lie our Herodotus and
Lepsius and the learned English pair.
There, too, we blot in our mockeries of the
glory about us in water colour, or Eugenio
tears the crimsoning curtain of evening
from its place to hang before his canvas.
There comes the coffee, which says, Ah!
after our Egyptian flesh-pots; and there

Kief has its throne sitting in the fragrant pipe-bowl. There too we review our heavenly host, questioning it for that Cross which carries with it the prediction of the true faith to benighted nations. It is our throne for the Nile voyage; from it the sight sweeps over the inexpressible sweetness of the green which breaks its sea of verdure at the base of the hills of Lybia, literally commanding the valley of the Nile; and doubly fortunate are we, for the river, now in flood, gives our sight its utmost scope.

After the oars came the sail; we did not go very far this first day, glad enough to go at all, for the breeze has been adverse for three weeks. It was uncertain weather for Egypt, and just before we left even a little rain fell. It seemed like the drops of good-bye wafted over the sea from eyes at home, so unnatural are raindrops here. Some thirty miles up the river we arrived, and did so without knowing it: a push into the soft mud bank, the four-clawed anchor dropped for a moment till we drive a post for our mooring-rope in the soft bank above us, and there we are. We can hit no rock, for there is none, to touch bottom is only the concern of a moment, ports there are none also ; so we simply lie against the bank, to which we step over a blue plank, while the Arabs hold up a hand-rail to guide us.

But this first night we did nothing of this, we were too absorbed in the intricacies of Antonio's *cuisine*, too new to our dahabeah to care to leave it. Antonio stamped his merits into our memory by one or two brilliant flourishes. His dates stuffed with almonds contributed to make Egypt better understood, and his coffee breathed from the bushes of Arabia Felix dream and enchantment. We slept well, and were early on deck to see the double panorama of either bank unrolling itself like a ribbon before our eyes. At least one side was always near enough for a landscape effect, and out came our sketch-books, and we shot manfully away, too often, alas! in a Parthian fashion, at the picturesqueness which fled from us. But I secured a belted minaret, a flight of steps, a few flat walls, a dab or two for figures, and thought it all wonderful.

By night we were at Benisouéf, our first town. These second-class Egyptian towns are chiefly built of sunburnt brick, and in square roofless blocks, which themselves look like gigantic bricks. The colour is a sober yellow-brown, very quiet and pleasant for sketching in light and shadow; looking mournful and squalid, but I suspect cool and comfortable as would be no other houses here. Sometimes pottery is let into the earth, which gives it a jewelled and fanciful appearance, and sometimes the interior of the rooms is whitewashed to make them light. But over the squalidest village, the meanest hut, stoops a king in compassionate fellowship, and where the palm is we are compelled to acknowledge a royal presence

which saves poverty from its abjectness. We had done, against the current, something like forty-five miles, which was a fair beginning. The next day the sky began to clarify, and these ghostly films of clouds, which, like a frown on a child's face, mean so little, were smoothing into that deep thoughtful brow of Egyptian day, in which so much of the world's earliest wisdom was thought out. We lapped this sunshine with our northern nerves and felt a little like the men about us, felt a little of that mind-growth which makes this river a paragon for what it does for the harvest of thought as of the field. We made four days to Minieh which sometimes, through baffling winds, extends to four times that length, and it was all delightful! a modest prelude to the grand things to come; a deep, simple, mournful music, like that with which the Arabs welcomed us to their Nile after our first meal; a grand monotony, which had the simplicity and weight of Bible words.

Few colours, the earth a golden brown, villages of no other colour, save where some white dome or shaft-like minaret sparkled above the acacia trees,—long horizontals almost architecturally bounding the borders of our Egyptian cup,— vertical lines cutting into great blocks of mountains, whose shadows, softly firm, gave character and energy everywhere; between the river and these grand cliffs, always, alone or in groups, the palm, an incomparable foreground, with its stem upright where an upright was needed, and its rich strong leaves telling against the golden shadowy hills; figures of men and women marvellously accented against the brightness, their deep blue dresses invaluable as emphasis where all is sunshine; the few animals,—the appealing and mournful buffalo, and the grand twisted camel silhouetted against the sunset like the genius of the desert; of such as these consists the picture which hourly unrolls itself before our delighted eyes.

Minieh wasn't much. We were detained a day there by a head wind. Eugenio and I made sketches after breakfast, and the ladies visited the market and reported enthusiastically of a beautiful girl they had seen in one of the houses. I had a walk with the fair English girl, and examined details of agriculture, seeing that most venerable of spectacles, a brown Egyptian holding his plough, so antique in form, with its team—a buffalo and a camel; the yoke is a straight beam and keeps the cattle very wide apart; the plough is a sensible enough looking plough, and its share at least is shod with iron. We saw, too, another fine old wonder, an Egyptian making his bricks with stubble, not having any straw. He strikes the soft earth, which is so fine that it binds, though certainly not clay, into a box without top or bottom, and lets the bricks dry in the sun in rows.

The sight of head-shaving is very entertaining. Samson's hair was certainly cut off with a razor, and probably a razor very like our own. These Egyptian razors must be sharp indeed, for they reap the hair like grain, and without any soap. The walks about the country are mostly slender dykes raised above the flats, and sometimes small patches have, as one formerly prepared the copper for etching, a little rim to contain the overflow.

December 1st.

Each dahabeah did a little shooting this morning, and a few hoopoos and pigeons were the result; ours when cooked were excellent, but I begin to believe that Antonio could travesty a crocodile into delightfulness. To-day we sailed famously, sixty miles; sweeping by the emerald plains, sharply varied at times with the new-ploughed earth, looking like a bronzed velvet; a distance of arid Lybian mountains, whence, in fancy, we could hear the roar of lions, till towards evening,

to our surprise, we found ourselves under
the battlemented cliffs fringing the water
on one side, and old Nile, terrible with
restricted energy, reduced to less than half
its usual size. Here, as the wind was
favourable, and the current strong, great
waves formed themselves as we crossed
the river to get the benefit of the smoother
margin, which we descended for a long
way. We almost swept the tall cliffs with
our burgee as we glided by. After a
while we left the cliffs, and by nightfall
reached Asyoot. The *Clara* came to our
assistance, as we caught badly in the mud,
her men joining with ours in pulling us
out of our troubles. In drawing the boat,
the men pass a slender loop over their
breast, which converges to a point where
it meets the stout rope which pulls us.
Thus harnessed they look like the old
Egyptians drawing the stones of the
Pyramids, which probably was done in
the same way.

Asyoot, December 2d.

A day of delights. Most faultless weather, in which repose and activity can be equally enjoyed, and we had both in perfection. Asyoot is by far the prettiest city we have seen ; so neat and shapely, stately with its seventeen minarets, and with a little suburb of domes and frost-like tracery, and superb palms, as if it were a poem by some Arabian poet. Our first thought was for the tombs in the cliffs overlooking the town, which were to be our first interview with Egyptian sculpture in site. A fine lot of little donkeys with their fruity saddles, like monstrous dates, and as usual, I found a countryman in my donkey. "Yankee Dood" seems ubiquitous in Egypt, and generally is a pretty good beast. The road was wonderfully good, and after a little trotting and galloping, in less than an hour we found ourselves at the tombs of Lycopolis. It must have come hard to make a deity out

of that scoundrel—the wolf; but the old
Egyptians apparently accepted the deity
as the author of evil as well as good,—all
life indeed being a part of himself, for had
we not just before swept under the high
chambers of the mummied crocodiles of
Beni Hassan?   But we saw no signs of
the wolf, nor a mummy of any sort, only
great doorways to mysterious tombs, on
which were cut gigantic forms of kings,
and processions of figures and animals.
This first sight of Egyptian work was very
impressive.   This intaglio, as they use it,
expresses with great purity of form and
line something of modelling and expression which we had not expected.   We saw
birds and beasts delicately cut, which we
instantly recognised ; they had something
of that naïf directness of intention which
gives the charm to Japanese drawings.
They evidently, like the Japanese, loved
the outline, and as the Japanese shirk the
imitation of the human countenance and
its expression, so did the Egyptians.   The

Egyptians draw a figure in profile, with the eye and shoulder as in a front view, and a full face of the Japanese has a nose without shadow, and a mouth like a blown rose-leaf. But each nation was a great artist in its way; both fully felt the value of the outline. The Japanese—for time is nothing in these things—is the Egyptian of to-day.

But oh, that view from the cavern's mouth! well may the Prophet have borne in his heart some legend of Egypt which lives yet in the verses of our hymn-book :—

> "Fair fields across the swelling flood,
>   Stand dressed in living green."

Never was there such a swelling flood,—never such a living green. And that rosy barrier of mountains beyond, how to the parched child of the desert must they seem as the Delectable mountains, beyond whose limit is the heavenly city and bliss ineffable!

After the tombs came the bazaar.

THE EARLY TYPE.

There, in that shadowy defile of glazed and harmonised colour, we turned aside to admire the masterpieces of Asyoot—its pipe-bowls and pottery. We saw a whole pipe-bowl carried forward from a handful of Nile mud to the polished and chased beauty we purchased ; nor could we resist a black water-bottle, which might have stood upon Cleopatra's supper-table for grace and elegance, and costing but two francs. We had some difficulty for our smelling-salts, but secured enough at last for the ladies, while, next door, a shop of the Bible Society furnished our unsancti-fied dahabeah with what, for the first time in our lives, we can use for an earthly as well as a heavenly guide-book. We met in the market-place the American Consul, who was a placid Arab, and looked as if he knew as little of America as we of the phœnix. He politely invited us to take coffee at his house, which we as politely declined, having unshaken faith in Antonio.

The evening before we had had an adventure. Soon after our arrival, the ladies, in stumbling over the town with the Fair One and her two Arabs with the lanterns, had received a street invitation to enter and see the ghawazee. They entered, not knowing where they went, and thinking the spacious room they were in a café, they even offered to fee one of the gentlemen, mistaking him, as did Tony Lumpkin, for a waiter. They were received with great courtesy by a number of gentlemen, who rose to greet them, and coffee was brought. Then the ghawazee danced. As rumour came flying to me of the adventure, I hurried to share in it. Before I reached the house, however, I saw the two long lanterns and figures that loomed gigantic in the obscurity. Our ladies had passed the ordeal of this Paphos of the Nile with becoming courage and satisfaction, and leaving them to go back, and taking from them Eugenio, I went in. The girls were again trotted out, apparently for my benefit. The place was no café, but a private house, that of the

Governor-General of Upper Egypt! A divan ran along two sides of the long hall, and on it were the company invited by our host on the occasion of his daughter's marriage. This is a common custom in Egypt, and sometimes the day before the gentlemen have their dancing-girls, the bride receives them among her friends.

After the Howadgi and so many more, I shall say nothing of the manner of dancing of these girls. There were only two—one, a genuine Egyptian type, handsome and tall; the other with a bad brand upon her brow, and nothing alluring in her looks. It was something, while smoking a cigarette on this second day of December, to be seeing Herodias dancing, and the girls of Gades, whom Juvenal describes, whose descendants still keep it alive in Spain's chachucha; something to look into that mysterious face, and the placid intensity of its smile, as the figure hovered nearer and nearer with musical and outstretched arms, like some bird hovering over its beloved;

something to see that great breastplate of coin—those face-pieces of gold, alone brilliant in the twilight, as when the dusky Egyptian night reclines, softly smiling, against the burnished splendours of the sun who makes way for her. It was Egypt all over, and we poor Howadgi of the north were there again to be fooled if we chose by this later Cleopatra, as long since, on this very river, was Marc Antony, and by a beauty not more fatally Egyptian than this. We were disappointed somewhat in the dress of the ghawazee. Instead of the ample *shintyan* and hanging sleeves we had heard of, she wore a belt around her waist, and her European dress descended to the floor ; but about the head and breast she was splendid ; by either cheek hung a *plaque* of coins—a perfect breastplate in front; and behind, braided in her hair, which fell to her waist, smaller coins, which shone like stars against the night of her tresses. They played small castanets, of metal apparently, as they danced, and half-a-dozen performers in the corner gave a relish and local flavour by their savage accompaniment. One of the musicians came and played a solo for me on the kamángeh, a famous Egyptian instrument.

Thursday, December 3d.

For the first time, to-day the *Clara* beat us, and was bedded against her bank long before ourselves. The reasons were two-fold :—we being badly stuck in the mud, the *Clara* sent several men in her boat who remained, and the boat with us, which slowed our light craft ; and we stopped, by good luck, having missed two sailors, one of them the reis's brother, just in time for them to come on board. They had had a good run for it, and our reis was much depressed, thinking his brother might have done something wrong and been im-prisoned. When we met the *Porchers* in the evening they twitted us on our slow sailing. We took our customary stroll between the mighty lanterns, and young

England peered about for a village in the vague hope of more ghawazee.

It is unpleasant to chronicle misfortune, so I have deferred mention of a calamity which we hope may not prove serious. Water burst through some pipes, flooding all below, and damaging our stores. Ruskallah would have poured ashes on his head and rent his garments had he not been a Syrian and an Englishman ; but he spoke severely to the bland reis, whose oversight it was, who replied by not a word. Ruskallah Assouyan, born of a Syrian mother and an English father, is a veteran in the service of the Nile. He has a huge portfolio full of recommendations, and, oddly enough, in no one of them a word of dis-approval. Still, outside the pocket-book, I have heard of things which show he was not without the sly roguery of his order, but we like him, and mean to like him to the end. I engaged him at once at Alexandria for his pleasant ways, and he shows himself even more active and clever than I had hoped. He sits beside our companion-way in placid contemplation of his gains, and the bubble of his narghileh may be heard there at intervals from dawn to darkness; but he is coming out every day stronger in a new character—that of a sportsman; he scarcely misses anything, and to-day he has shot a wild goose, a zigzag, and a lovely ibis, snowy white, whose skin we mean to preserve for home embellishment. It was amusing to witness this mixture of sport and travel. We shouted to boys on the bank where the dead birds lay, and the magical "backsheesh" made them willing helpers. But the wild goose was only wounded, and on a lonely sand island; so we gentlemen and Ruskallah went ashore and had a run for him; he will be a treasure in Antonio's hands.

December 4th.

Like yesterday, our second cool day on the Nile. Our enemy, the fly, has disappeared. Now that he is gone let us abuse that vagabond. He is incredible. So intelligent and shameless that Beelzebub may well be his father. He puts intention into his nip, and manages to make it a personal affront. We feel as if it were Satan persecuting us for our sins, and there is no escape from him. He is in your cup—on your nose, at the same instant ; he is the able-bodied hereditary descendant of the plagues of Egypt, and every traveller is obliged to vote him a deliberate execration ere he has been long in Egypt. Whether it be that he and his ancestors have been stimulated by the virus of millenniums of infants' eyes, or that heat developes his native intelligence, he flies straight at your eye as can the fly of no other country, and he knows instantly when your hands are occupied, and redoubles his attacks. The common Egyptian women, with their children swung upon them, suffer them to hang heavy upon their youthful lids, wisely holding that they become blind if the flies are brushed off. For the same reason they do not wash their eyes; the consequence naturally is that we are always hitting against blind Calendars in the streets of Cairo, and a third of the population seem either one-eyed or sightless. To look at the creature there is nothing unusual in his appearance. The same pugnacious knobby head, hands that rub themselves in demoniac exultation, and those filmy coat-tails which might belong to a deacon, busy with good errands. He is rather smaller perhaps than our average fly, but small as he is, rightfully stands as head devil of Egypt. The mosquito is a Quaker to him; both his hum and sting are naught as compared to their New England brethren. Of other pests we almost know nothing; an occasional smart near the ankle reminds us that there are such things, and one day a band of gigantic but harmless wasps wove their waltz about our heads and departed as they came. Of course there are no rats in our dahabeah;

a vague rumour of one killed by an Egyptian ferret we purchased, remains unaccredited since the death of the ferret.

But to fly at higher game than flies—the birds of Egypt. The beautiful, blissful creatures! When one remembers that besides the native ones, so many northern birds we know and love find their winter homes here, we cannot wonder at their abundance. It is a marvellous sight to see them marshalling their lines against the sunset. Long streams of wild geese and wild ducks will unwind and snap their threaded length, like a whip, wheeling a thousand of them into line in a moment, and playing at cat's cradle against the smouldering day. Or a cloud of little birds will suddenly rise like a pinch of dust in the air, and as suddenly disappear; and the waders—the race of cranes and storks—will stand silent and silvery, tessellating some brown sand bar, with perhaps one unwieldy pelican as silent as themselves. And the raptores — always,

always overhead ˙can we see hanging in the sky the wicked vulture, its shaggy pin-feathers dark against the brightness.

The ibis is the sacred bird of Egypt—the destroyer of serpents in the caves of Lybia, as Herodotus says—or, as some say, loved of old Egypt for its hostility to locusts. We see plenty of a smaller white species; but I believe we have not as yet seen the bird sacred of old.* We have offended the gods by shooting one of the former kind, and it now hangs with expanded silver wings above our cabin door. May it not prove to us modern mariners an albatross, and bring a curse upon the *Rachel !* But the popular bird of Egypt is the pigeon or dove ; they build for it in every Nile village dove-cotes made of pottery, and looking like big bee-hives. The pigeons hover about every town, fearless in their evolutions ; and the aerial circuits of all birds in Egypt, in grace and playfulness,

* The sacred species is now only found on the Upper Nile beyond Kartoum.

D

are unmatched elsewhere. They will swing over a village, cutting figure eights in the air, and then a thousand, in one exquisite swoop, will dash upon the river, where for a while they will pause to drink. Such grace is there here of motion that even the heavy pelican, seemingly too unwieldy to fly, will in great numbers find a happy curve for their flight and unexpected buoyancy. They shine like ingots of silver against the gold of the sunset, as they sweep down the river. When one thinks that pigeons are one of the oldest birds of Egypt, and that the monuments represent them serving as carrier-pigeons do now, during the earlier dynasties, we feel for them a reverence mingled with our familiarity, which they deserve. Constantinople loves them, as does the Nile ; and Venice, deriving from Constantinople, fetches to Europe the pleasing superstition. The flock of St. Mark's Piazza shows us in little what Moslem countries offer so often.

We are unconscious generally of our daily departure and arrival, so easily are we afloat and so softly landed that our nerves often fail to apprehend either. To-day we have had a fresh wind, and the captain was off before we were up. We are sure of a fresh landscape every time we mount to our deck; the same general features, but so varied by changes in the heights of our two valley barriers, and their approach or recession from the Nile, and the almost incredible changes which all things undergo as the day proceeds, that the scene always has an air of novelty. Our valley barrier on the left, or Arabian side, is the only one which much changes its direction. But this in many places is a majestic wall of rosy sandstone, under which the Nile flows deep and dark. There are high-mark water lines, left we know not when, fifteen or twenty feet above the river. These rosy, golden cliffs, as morning or evening strikes, are belted with strata, fissured with vertical lines, and rounded into curves, which give a look of fantastic architecture, when all is natural —natural save where from our boat, high hung in air we see square punctures on the surface, and there, in their lofty chambers, the crocodiles and the wolves and the jackals of old Egypt slept a dreamless sleep within their pitchy shrouds. At times the rocks show us fantastic profiles. We have seen a sphynx and a lion; and how much the artists of old saw in these simple and grand forms the hint for their own architecture we can readily guess. Nothing that was not simple, nothing that was not massive, could stand before the grandeur of these cliffs; beside them the Parthenon would look finical, and the Minster of Strasburg a Gothic craze. In each country its architecture must be expressed by the nature which is most truly the flower of that race. He must find in his deep heart the answer to that yearning of man for nature's secret —his genius will be the culmination of nature's expression in the country where he lives. The artist is the go-between who explains this ideal to man; and here, in Egypt, truly found what nature tried to express. This silence, this grandeur, this mystery,—is it not everywhere? The murmur of adoring faith, which felt deeper than it knew, was it not whispered in the ear of the servant of Osiris in the intervals of the Memnonian silence of these desert barriers and the mystic wave which washes their feet?

Amid all the comfort and independence of our boat life, we are sometimes startlingly reminded of the heavy hand of tyranny which weighs upon Egypt behind its smiling azure. The other day, towards sunset, we saw a swart and drowned Egyptian sweeping onward with the current; he may have come from miles up the river. All avoided him—to be cognisant of a fatal deed under a tyranny is sometimes to be a participant in it. The pity therefore which would save the dying or bury the dead is denied by the instinct of self-preservation.   And so the body fled to Cairo, where some officer of the government may hear of it, and give it the rest that it longs for.   Where is the coroner's inquest, where the newspaper article, which will not let such a thing pass in darkness ?   Alas ! such things here never have been and may never be.   The word human rights probably has no equivalent in Arabic ; the right of representation Egypt is no nearer now than in the days of her Ptolemys ; we have entered that East where a king has always been a despot, and where not alone pyramids demanded hundreds of thousands of hands to build up the glory of one king.   Everywhere it is some Rameses, some conqueror, some satrap above, and the millions of unconsidered people below.   By all with whom I have talked here of giving to the fellah more freedom, I have always been told that it was impossible—that he could not bear liberty, and would abuse it.   A nation of slaves since the dawn of history would find the pure waters of liberty an intoxicating draught; and yet one cannot help a kind of sympathy with the few efforts that have been made to shake off the yoke here.

The evening before we were shown, as we swept under noble cliffs which almost reached the river, a village which had been the centre of disaffection and revolt. A chief had mustered some ten thousand men to assert themselves against the government; what they managed to do, however, was to attack an English boat passing this town, and kill the reis, who had barricaded himself in his cabin. The khedive instantly surrounded them by land and water, and dispersed them with slaughter. Our dragoman said he was only two miles up the river at the time this happened; he thought the rebels sacrificed were as many as two thousand.*

* Perhaps only a dragoman's story as to numbers. A dragoman sees what he thinks you wish to see, and

The *Clara* led us all day, as we surrendered to the fascinations of sport; but
in the evening we overtook her, and soon
after dark she nestled at our side, beyond
the long line of native boats.

Girgeh, Saturday, 5th.

This is a flourishing commercial town,
exporting much wheat.   For the reason
that it is good and cheap, it is the usual
stopping place for bread-making.   Half of
our men were off by dawn to do this.
They buy the corn, grind it, make it into
bread, and store it, all in one day.   The
men feed themselves, as is the habit of
the river boats; economy, therefore, with
them is important.   They sit on the deck,
elbow to elbow, in a close circle around
their grand old Pharaonic wooden bowl,
not dipping their fingers in the dish as
usually do Orientals, but using handsome
black spoons of wood.   They dry their

says what he thinks enhances his own and his river's
importance.   My journal often talks like a dragoman.

bread in the sun to prevent its moulding;
this is done aft, and our steersman looks
the picture of plenty as he stands up to his
knees in bread-chips. We sometimes take
up one and throw it to the hungry naked
boys, who run on the river brink and
make little cart-wheels and hand-springs
for backsheesh. Ruskallah was off at
dawn for shooting, but soon returned
with an empty game-bag.

After breakfast, preceded by Abdallah
and his wand of office, we walked through
the town, visiting the bazaar, which was
not splendid. The best thing we saw
was a school. Going up narrow stairs
to a front room, we found some forty
Mohammedan boys all reciting their Coran
verses to the placid and nut-brown domi-
nie, while sundry erudite little scholars
were reading their Arabic in wicker-
work supports made to hold a book. I
was delightfully reminded of Decamps'
picture of the same subject. I have heard
that he never went beyond Smyrna, and

where an extinct priesthood have written their services upon many a rock-altar, under a roof of perfect azure surely not made by human hands.

And the labours of our dahabeah must go on ; our miracle-monger, Antonio, at the boat's bow, must continue his leger-demain, by producing dishes apparently out of nothing, and the sailors can know no Sunday under their urgency of labour ; but they never forget their prayers.   It is a beautiful and humiliating sight for us, slaves of a day and a place, to see them, without formality thrice in the day facing the East, bow themselves to the deck in adoration.   It seems to me the truest form of worship ; held anywhere under the broad sky in the midst of labour and unashamed before man.   And it is always respected ; its simple dignity finds a place in the midst of the con-fusion and labour of life.   I have seen a sailor, in spite of our marine evolutions, silent, praying in the hubbub, unreproached by any. And they do this three times a day. Wonderful mystery of man's nature that can find in this valley rest and faith for so many beliefs! A simple ejaculation of ignorant souls, who, in spite of it, can rise to the level of neither truth nor honesty.

And Ruskallah, the cosmopolite, is unbound by any faith in particular apparently. As our wind was languid to-day, which we opened with the humiliation of poleing, Ruskallah went on shore with an Arab for shooting. He has just returned with his trophies, consisting of a little zig-zag, so pretty with its tuft, half-a-dozen pigeons, and a large wader, which the Arabs will not kill because its cry resembles holy words. He calls it "caravan," but I as yet have not found it in our book of Egyptian birds. This morning we shot into a group of hideous vultures, but they were too tough for our shot. Mr. Porcher, more successful, yesterday killed an eagle.

December 7th

A windless day. Earth and sky make one great globe of light with an equatorial belt of dark, enough to hold the two together. One even better studies the gradations of the sky in their reflections in the water; which is brighter, sky or water, it is hard to say. The river has more lustre, the sky more depth; there is certainly less glow in the water, and Eugenio tells me that water is always less light than sky in tone, though it is sometimes hard to see it.

If the word "Egypt" had a mystic derivation it should be—light. Light is its characteristic; other skies, like that of Rome, have glow and softness, and others, like our own, glow and hardness; but Egypt is light. So subtle is the air that distances are marked by an aerial delicacy, which, acting upon the simplicity of the forms, gives the landscape its grace and grandeur, and this same light acts upon us after our fashion as it does upon the valley about us. We feel along every nerve the ascent of the sun to its culmination, and every film of shadow which gauzes the cliffs about us as he descends, throws its peace also upon our dazzled spirits. We could tell the time of the day by our sensations, and these, indeed, are our clock here; no two watches agree, and there is nothing to regulate them; they are away like prodigal sons from the great minster clocks which kept them in order at home, and at last, even their partial owners learn to disbelieve in them. But our nerves are true time-keepers; they make us jump from our narrow couches at sunrise to enjoy the delightfully cool bath, or to wander away with a gun on our shoulder for game and exercise. Midday, says sunstroke, in a voice too loud to be disobeyed; but it is evening, the famous twilight which must have made the Sun God so prominent among the deities of old, for then it is not only the eye that sees such chastened splendours that the brightest colour has its sobriety, but something more falls out of heaven upon us which trans- figures our souls. The peace that smooths the way of the setting sun reaches us ; we are a part of the pageant, and that hour so inexpressibly tender and holy, stills us in adoring rapture, till, as the last ember dies, we arise from our spiritual intoxication with a sigh.

We wandered about the fields after break- fast, and came upon the famous doura in full bearing. It is a plant curiously like our corn, of the same height and of slender leaves, which fall backward on themselves, but, instead of the ear of corn, one great knob of grain there is to each plant. Each kernel of this grain looks like a diminutive corn-kernel, and tastes not unlike it ; it is the staple food of the fellaheen. I only wonder that no one has tried it in America.

In all their misery the fellaheen are a stalwart race. One can't be much mis- taken as to the health and muscularity of people whom we daily see in familiar nudity. And this grain must have much contributed to this ; let our farmers' clubs look to the matter.

The *Clara* people looked in on us to see the birds we had shot. The sic-sac, which we so naturally called "zig-zag," proves to be a plover, and the classic trochilus of Herodotus, who relieves the crocodile's mouth of leeches ; only some dreadful savants will have it there are no leeches in the Nile. I, in return, went to see Mr. Porcher's eagle ; it was a young one, and looked less like an eagle than a hawk ; its bill was longer, with a lesser curve, and the grand arch of bone which protects its eye from the sun, oddly enough, was wholly wanting. Perhaps it would have developed later, when older.

A pleasant freshness enters the window— a visitor from the far north of ice and newspapers—and in a minute our reis has pushed us from the bank, and old Nilus is playing his pleasant music against our sides.

E

The breeze held pleasantly, and we made up for our delays, but at night we had a misadventure just at a spot where a branch of the Nile came pouring into the main river in strong eddies. Two native boats got in our way, then came the *Clara*, for whom we made room, and then the current swung our head round ; this it did twice in spite of anchoring, so that we had, after an hour's delay, finally to track it. By this time it was dark and cold, yet our sailors merrily leaped into the water, and laughed as they laboured at the rope. They waded across the broad branch of the Nile, the cause of our disaster. It was strange to hear their wild cries while their figures disappeared ; as the file stretched deeper and deeper in the water, it reminded me of Pharaoh's soldiers and his engulphed host. Soon we were all right, with a fine midnight breeze blowing due aft. How soundly we slept after all our anxiety !

Tuesday, 8th.

At dawn we found we had regained our consort and the Russian boat, which proves to be a Prussian one. Our dragoman says one of the Emperor's sons is in it,* a fine-looking youth, who shows his blood-thirsty Prussian ways by incessant shooting and dropping wounded doves, without recovering them, into the river.

The landscape about us has a character of space, and at times of beauty, we have not known before. The river sides, too, have changed their character; Arabia retreats and the Lybian hills have come to the front; they are more serrated than the Arabian, less like a gigantic platform of rock.

There is no sunshine without its shadow, and the troubles of life are made more poignant by its delights. To-day weighed heavily upon us; we depend upon the breeze for coolness, and that failed us.

* A dragoman's inaccuracy.

While our sailors tracked wearily in the blazing sunshine, we, under an awning, were as uncomfortable as they, and the flies knew we were down, and hit us accordingly. Their life is annoyance, and the sun stimulates this to inconceivable activity. Better a Lybian lion alone on his sandhill than one of these wretches. Their feet are shod with fire, their kiss is poison. Vainly did we strew our fly-paper with their corpses; *semper at que recurrit.*

Our reading power melted from us. I could only touch up my sketch of the ghawazee which I had made two days before. We found a village specimen not far from our boat, and she accepted our invitation to come on board. She called herself a ghawazee, and looked it. There is certainly something gipsyish in the three specimens I have seen. This one at an English fair would not look out of place, and the ghawazees claim to be gipsies. This one could not dance much, but posed divinely. She wore a dark-blue dress, with

a circlet of blue and white below her neck, and her dress had a chequer-work of crimson. We asked her age. She said she did not know it. Her manners had the same dreamy grace so common with Arabs, who seem to have wandered to us out of dreams.

What a blessing was the coming on of night! We enthusiastically repeated as the freshness fell on us out of Heaven,

" From the cool cisterns of the midnight air,
My spirit drank repose."

It was health after a fever ; and when we pushed into a bank, under a magnificent grove of palms, we were quite ready for a walk. What a walk it was! We had never seen such a landscape before in Egypt. As far as sight could reach, from our feet a carpet of tender green—wheat probably—extended, from which rose a palm-grove, whose beautiful green was made sombre by contrast. We were at Ballas, famous for its earthern jars called

Ballasee, with which we had met many boats freighted on the river. The town looked like a Golgotha — a lovely one indeed — for great heaps of jars were everywhere, and in the distance they resemble skulls. We skirted the town, and wandered into the fragrant meadows beyond. We spoke softly, the kàttar khéirak of salutation to passing Arabs — were followed by our usual crowd of juvenile nudities, half-brave and half-timid, till, from a mighty wave of Abdallah's baton, they fled in comic terror. We paused to caress a little black lamb, with the prettiest silver tip to its tail, and a tiny donkey, which an urchin pushed along as if it were a toy; I think, indeed, I have seen as large a one in Giroux's toy department.

Turning our heads as we came away, we saw evening behind us—a blaze of saffron and gold, against which rose the houses of cold grey with their dove-cots, from whose tops boughs extended. Beyond them, the violet hills, and in front a wild dash of bronze-green, with shadowy figures in cold, pale blue, moving hither and thither, made a landscape we can never forget. We returned with a capital appetite for our capital dinner. Antonio is inexhaustible. If we could do our part as he his, there would be nothing to regret. We noticed that our sailors had stuck a knife, against the jettatura of the seated saint we left without visiting, into the mast. Just as we had finished dinner, we were called out to see Ruskallah's struggles with an enormous fish. I felt his line, and he certainly was there. We let down a boat for him, and soon saw the monster sprawling on the deck; he may have weighed twenty-five pounds, which is, for a river fish, heavy; he is called armoot. He was cut in two, and one-half given to the sailors. We have eaten a little one before, and found it good.

9th December.

Even we were not without our interest

in the transit of Venus, and close by us at Thebes there are watchful observers. As our German prince is gone on, we think he may have hurried to see the transit scientifically. We went to bed quite sure of one thing, that whatever might happen, there would be no clouds; so we were up before sunrise, with our noses pressed against the smoked glass, and waiting for the transit. I have sacrificed my window-pane for the advance of science, and almost to our surprise (for one can never get familiar with man's stupendous power of anticipating God's intention in such matters), there it was, a visible spot of dark upon the luminous disk. And it was delightful to be seeing this in Egypt. It has been said that we can never truly know Egyptian chronology till we can read their records of eclipses. If they had stumbled on the lens, what would there have been for us of later days to find out? And it would surprise nobody if we yet found a telescope in an Egyptian tomb.

The windings of the river made our wind a side one, and I was only surprised to see how near our boat could sail to it. But we had to track; we overtook our Prussian prince, and got badly mixed up with him. In dodging shadoofs and shore huts, our ropes jerked together, and he being already aground, we were delayed. But the poor *Clara* could not take advantage of our bad luck, for she was invisible around a bend of the river. At last the prince was off, and slanting across the river, showed us his heels. His finest piece of game, so to say, is a magnificent eagle, very unlike Mr. Porcher's. Of this, it may indeed be said that he has

.   .   .   . " the strength of pinion
That the Theban eagle bear "   .   .   .

for is he not a Theban eagle ?

At last the white sails of the *Clara* slowly crept into sight. How beautiful are these sails of a dahabeah !——the long taper yard, so long that it is always spliced at the lower end, and of a wood brought here from Europe; the outer sail line a curve which would have rendered Hogarth frantic with delight, and the snowy expanse of the sail always suggesting two things—a bird's wing and the leaf of the sword-lily. I am proud to have discovered this latter resemblance, which all confess to be admirably true.

The mystery of the pivot of the short mast, on which the yard turns, and that quickly, I have not yet solved, but when we descend the river the long yard will be removed and placed in rests overhead, we then using only the smaller sail aft,—then I shall understand it. A man sits always holding the sheet, which the sail draws; when a squall strikes her, he lets it fly, for we have no reefing. This is necessary for safety, as it would be impossible that a boat should have much draught or a keel where there are so many mud-banks.

But perhaps the finest poetry of the sail is felt at night when we furl it. To do this the whole crew slowly creep along this yard, some sixty feet long, in the gathering darkness. To see their dusky figures printed against the palpitating splendour of the stars—the farthest seen through the twilight seeming incredibly far—is a sight which every evening fills us with wonder. How they do it I cannot understand; but I plainly see that they walk up the masts, with their bare feet on cleets, which serve as a ladder.

We heard the guns of Luxor's consuls welcoming the prince, and very soon we were as loudly welcomed, which Ruskallah returned by the discharge of everything on board, till he came to his revolver, which refused to waste powder so foolishly. We had just time to step ashore, and stand for a moment in the twilight, face to face with those grand old lines which make a millennium of years as yesterday, before we were called back to our dinner. With deep awe and wonder, we had felt everything converging to this glory of the

Thebaid, as we drew near. The mountain-chains on either side, grander in form than ever, their evening hue of violet tenderer than ever, seemed to approach the river as for a festival; and as we came by, glimpses which took away our breath, were caught of obelisks—those columns, whose forms we know so well—a colossal prince, who sat as if enchanted under the Lybian mountains; and finally, far in the west, the mysterious pair — sublime in their indistinct simplicity—were caught and lost by turns, and over the Colossi a great crimson wing of sunset waved us to our place of rest. It was Luxor.

But two or three places on earth can rival the overwhelming interest it has. It was well with *Rachel*. She found herself, and later the *Clara* nestled beside her, under these immemorial walls. We were too full of content to be quite quiet. Our rest was restless, and we longed for the morrow. Our worthy consul, with a proffer of his own donkey for the visit to

SITTING ON THE HEELS.

Karnak, and good ones for the ladies, paid us a visit of ceremony. Little does he probably know if America be an island or a continent, but he knew that our coffee was good, and we gave him the pipe of friendship, and he told us the last news of Luxor. A row of young Egyptians were sitting on their heels on the bank, in respectful admiration of our interview, and that very attitude is on the sculptures about us ; and the little drum which our men strike with their hand, while our sailors sing that song we love so much—in its minor key like some touching wail heard down the centuries—can we not see that same drum struck by the same brown hands cut by some artist five thousand years ago ?

December 10, Luxor.

The ardent Eugenio was off at dawn in our sandal to make a sketch of the ruins from the river, and grand and impressive was the sketch he brought back to us—of that brown which, whether man or building, is so Egyptian, save in the corner of his sketch, where the wave quivered under the already fiery kisses of the rising sun. Above us, on the bank, are the huts and tents of the scientific party. How beautiful last night was the long line of lamps, along their yard and side—man's humble return for the celestial pageant it celebrated. The *Clara* has friends among them, and paid them a visit, but after their severe labour and excitement they were cooling off in their bath. Of the party, it seems an amateur has the finest instrument, but as yet we hear nothing of what they have discovered. His name is Colonel Campbell, and his dahabeah is one of the largest and finest on the Nile; it is externally adorned with palm branches quite beautifully.

Since writing the above, we have visited his tent, and seen his noble instrument. It rests upon a massive stone which he brought from England. They have a little field-glass through which they practise looking, to be sure of precision. The day of the observation was especially suitable, and one savant had a photographic apparatus which fired second-shots at the sun through the whole time. Here the sun at his rising had Venus nearly across his limb. Those savants four or five hours farther east must have seen the whole transit.

Off Erment, Monday, December 14th.

At last we are again afloat, and how soothing is this rippling water and our tented deck after the burden of such a weight of centuries upon the brain! We have been five days at Luxor—four of them of hard work, and one of needed repose. Fortunately for us the weather was cool though windless, and our fatigue was more of the mind than of the body. Valiantly throwing off the bondage of Murray, who advises the contrary, we began with Karnak. Our American consul, a stately

Arab, sent me his own donkey. He was a superb creature, with housings about the head of purple and gold, and his back was sheeted with crimson; but his officious donkey-boy half-spoiled him for me by jabbing him with a steel-pointed stick, and upbraiding his impenitence with all the yells of Arabia. It was not till I had got his stick away, and had silenced his cries, that I could enjoy my splendid mount. And then how pleasant it was to wander away with our little caravan across these plains, which look endless, and to know that behind yonder palms waits for us the wonder of the world—that sacred city whose ruins are the humiliation and almost the terror of our own day.

After half-an-hour we entered the vast open gate—one of the finest of those entrances to the temples which gave Thebes the epithet of the hundred-gated—but not city-gates. There never was a wall to the city, and these hundred gates admitted to what we can even now see to have been the grandest chain of temples, the scene of man's highest achievement in religious architecture. Though the Egyptians had the arch both round and pointed, the horizontal line was the inevitable expression of their genius. What a huge block was that which made the top of this doorway. How high hung in air, and how far grander was it all than the low, clumsy triumphal arch of Rome at its best! One's spirit was lifted to enter by such a portal. And then everywhere that profusion of figures on the surface, infinite simplicity and infinite detail. The avenue of sphinxes made no impression; so close together were they; so, as it were, beneath our feet; so mutilated, we could not judge them—we did not even try to do it; but when later, on a wall, we saw cut the flowing lines and majestic human face of a sphinx, we know what they must have been. Soon, breathless with surprise, we stood in the great hall of Karnak. We could not look; we could only feel. So

unaccustomed were we to such grandeur
that we did not essay to take in the proportions of the temple, but sat amid this
wreck of the Titans, and dreamily looked
on and on, past many a fallen, many a
standing, column, till our eye rested upon
the sunshine of another temple-gate, so far
away it seemed to be impossible that it
should be a gate of Karnak.

Though we visited Karnak twice, we
did not possess it. The unaccustomed
nobleness of style—our ignorance of what
each hall or colonnade might mean, and
the cruel overthrow of these astonishing
masses, made it impossible for our minds
to possess them. When we again could
revise our Lepsius, our Martineau, our
Wilkinson, could we with learned accuracy
find the names for what we have seen, but
sitting there, all was fused in the sentiment
of ruined grandeur. And soon to know
yet more ruin; in the first hall, every
column but one had fallen; some slipped
from the first drum, and others incredibly

snapped across, only one majestic survivor showing what they have been. I noticed that Nature, even when destructive, feels a touch of pity, and leaves for us enough beauty, with imagination's help, to complete the rest. We looked down with anger upon our slippery flooring, and almost hated the Nile for doing all this. He it is that sends his annual flood, baleful with poisonous nitre, to sap these columns the ages had spared for us, and soon must they all lie in dreadful confusion, while the wicked wave shall tear the beauty of their priceless lines. A sea-wall of burnt brick costing little, would, perhaps, save for us the beauty of Karnak.* Let Christendom give the paltry sum, and see that the Khedive protects what the ages have entrusted to him. A certain picturesqueness, from the strange position of half-fallen columns, some standing inclined and golden against the blue

* I find that the Nile, by infiltration through the soil, cannot be stayed—so that the doom of Karnak is as sure as it is immediate.

sky, and some heavily resting upon the
shoulders of their upright brothers, have
an effect in utter contrast to the architect's
intention.

After all, this architecture consists only
of temples, with upright walls, or sometimes inclined, and colonnades of columns
not lofty, their capitals but variations of the
line of the bud and flower of the lotus and
papyrus. In this rainless country they
needed no steep roof, therefore the towering Gothic aisle was impossible, and the
columns had to be close together for the flat
slab to reach across. Light was not needed ;
it is in excess ; and the old windows, of
which we saw several examples, had heavy
stone upright bars, but none across, for they
needed not glass. Oddly enough, one of
the first things we saw at Luxor was a
cross ; the meaning of it we did not know,
but there it was, seeming to say — your
cross is mine, for I planted the seed of
the sublime ethics which, stolen and trans-
planted in Judea by Moses, in the fulness of

time flowered into the loveliness of Christ. But the figures in the temples far surpassed in august beauty our expectations. They move before our eyes a procession of spirits stripped of materialism and fastuous colour, friendly yet remote, half imparting and half hiding their secret. They all have the beauty of adolescents, and spring forward with an energy which is only suppressed. There is not a child or an old man among them; they are the ideal of human life—youthful manhood. The immortal life of the hereafter blooms calm and everlasting upon each face, and their sweet close smile is the smile of present happiness; the brow is full, the eyes wide apart and heavy-lidded, their nose a delicate aquiline, their chin small and short. The whole countenance breathes spiritual loveliness, and even their great conquerors, from their chariots slaughtering and trampling their enemies, bend their bows, or wave their falchions, as in celestial calm; no frown disfigures their brows, and the same sweet smile we know so well is on their lips. They reminded me of the Apollo watching the flight of his arrows, only his grace is that of a phthisical dandy compared with these. And we saw the trains of captives, with the thongs about their wrists, made little, as men so situated feel, and at Medînet Haboo we saw those captive Jews which link this land with our Bible.

So, at last, saturated, overwhelmed, as if time had presented us with a goblet too heavy for our weak nerves, we returned, jaded and joyous, to our dahabeah. Groups of palms printed their feathery architecture against the sunset, to show us in this full Egypt how all Nature's hints had not been appropriated, while over the little lake at their feet, flights of silvery ibises circled mysteriously. It was the evening's and the Nile's hour of worship, and gladly from our divans we watched and shared it, continuing the new adoration we had found at Karnak. Almighty Amun Ra looked sweetly at us, and we became in soul

Egyptians, and mystery floated to us from the far tombs of Medînet Haboo on the twilight, while glistening Nilus, darkening in his banks, counted his flocks of birds in chaplets, as beadsmen do their beads. And calm fell upon us out of heaven, and we were at peace.

We divided our work into alternate days on either side of the river, and so the second day we visited the Colossi. We had to take donkeys twice, crossing a little arm of the Nile in a stupendous boat, consisting of irregular chunks of unpainted wood, and the oars crooked tree-boughs. And our ghostly, tattered oarsman might well have been the original Egyptian Charon taking us to the Elysian fields and the dead of old. It is still the constant custom here for the dead to cross the Nile and be buried at home, and the old Egyptians always carried a corpse over an artificial lake, called the Lake of the Dead; and through these legends Charon first came from Greece to Italy.

We saw one of these boats, just at our boat's bow, starting with its freight of death. As the camel who bore the corpse was unladen, he lamented as never did hired mourner. They always wail and moan at the sight of a load ; their cry might be called the burden of the Desert, in the sense the word is used in Holy Writ. The scrambling of the donkeys out of the boat on the Theban side was as funny as their getting in. A few sprang over, but mostly went piecemeal, or were hoisted over like infants. Soon we were proudly careering over the level plain with our obligato suite of Scarabee-Arabs and bright little girls who ran by our side carrying water-pitchers for our lunch, and showing their faultless teeth, made whiter by their eyes of darkness. Of all gifts of bone or ivory which we could carry from Egypt we would most gladly take these pearly teeth ; even the very mummies have them ; no hot bread and sugary messes have spoiled for the earlier or later Egyptians their beautiful enamel. And so we rode through the streets of lupin, whose inexpressible green, and whose enchanting odour struck our senses with delight, watched by the guardians of the plain and of the mystic city behind them.

These great Twin Brethren are the only statues in Egypt whose situation is perfection. Others are lost in rubbish, or crowded against fallen column or propylon, but these sit secure in their solitude with the purple mountains behind them, and gazing with their sightless eyes at their brethren of Karnak. Shattered, defaced, featureless, they still look with a regal placidity through the disfigurement which somehow still keeps this expression. And they are just far enough apart; their seventy feet of height measures the space between them; it gives them privacy in companionship. Their simplicity was utter, nor could rent or fissure destroy it. Eugenio and I both tried our hand at sketches. It was perhaps better than

writing our names upon the base, and yet
so we should have been in illustrious company.   Famous kings and heroes, from the
golden days of Greece and Rome down
to the persistent snob of our own time,
are there all inscribed.   It may be per-
mitted for a royal personage on his travels
to perpetuate his joy at hearing. Memnon
once, twice, or thrice, but why Jenkins
should mention *his* existence in such company is incredible.   Though the insatiable
Yankee has written out his insignificance
everywhere by tar and paint-pot, I am
happy to say the first snob's name I saw
was not his, but a Frenchman's—one
Prichard, natif de Toulon, in majéscules.
Was he only coolly audacious, or did he
really enjoy the thought of every beholder's contemptuous loathing as he came
to it ?

  The music of Memnon, it is almost certain,
was caused by the disruption of particles
in its sandstone as the sun acted on the
moisture of the night.   An Arab clambered

up the statue's back, and struck it with a stone, when it resounded musically.

After the Colossi, Medînet Haboo. The remains of temples here, less oppressively sublime than those of Karnak, had fascinations of their own. They were of the good period, and their cuttings had that beautiful precision and *netteté* which Rome vainly attempted to rival. One of the most charming things here in the long corridors, was the blue ceilings of starry sky, still retaining their colours. The stars were all five-pointed, with three points on one side. And I stood where I could compare the blue of this sky with the real one beyond; they were wonderfully the same; the temple sky seemed a continuation of the one without. Eugenio and I outlined some heads of character, quite Jewish looking, at a conqueror's triumph; and the ladies wandered hither and thither, a whole world of enigma and suggestion inviting from the sculptured and painted world of creatures around them,

till satiated nature could no more.   Then
we gladly found ourselves between shadowy
columns, Arab fashion, seated on my beautiful rug, on which Paolo had spread our
lunch.   Nothing draughts life from one as
does such sightseeing,. a double activity of
mind and body.   How good did the plain
boiled eggs taste as we sat thus royally
with kings of old looking on, and like
Louis Fourteenth on his great public
dinner days, with our admiring crowd of
attentive courtiers.   And when the cigar
had wafted from us on its blue wave every
film of fatigue, to donkey again, and away
for the Memnonium, if possible more grand
and more exquisite than the ruin we
had left.   Hardly had we arrived before
Eugenio and I fell in love with a beautiful
gigantic head of basalt, which, polished as
at its hour of finish, retained the lustre of
its eye and the sunshine of its enchanting
smile.   But the mind, like a sponge, can
only hold just so much of even such an
element of delight, and we offered our

unresisting but weary bosoms to the soft
shock of a beauty and a grandeur we could
not fairly hold ; it slipped from us as things
escape us in a dream, and over the plain
again went we, little Fatmé still showing
her ivories, and chattering her pretty
English, till we reached the inevitable
boat, and were bundled into it as before.
It was like leaving the old civilisation for
the new, to find ourselves again bravely
rowing in our sandal under the stars and
stripes.

We had a visit from Mr. Smith, an
American, who has resided seventeen
years here. He is evidently a learned
man, and gave us a sketch of the old
religion, which was clear and precise.
Lady Duff Gordon has cruelly wronged
him, if one may trust the assertions of the
English and American Consuls, who gave
us as the reason for these slanders that he
was honester than the rest. We returned
his visit the morning after he called, and
found him living in the pleasantest house

in Luxor. He has a spacious terrace, whence he can overlook the emerald plain as far as the Pair, and a spacious garden, which he allowed the ladies to ravage. They brought home heaps of Egyptian roses of that faded dusky purple which the sun has made livid; the blossom of the henna, looking and smelling so like mignonette, and a camphor-plant, whose leaves are duplicated like the honeysuckle's. We have been in several Pashas' gardens along the river and seen there strange and lovely things, but this eternal absence of rain gives to shrubs and trees a weary look, as if they missed something—and they know no gardener, in the Scotch sense of the word. Those careless tangled alleys know no dainty female hand to trim them, nor echo to any female foot. Their chief use seems to be to furnish the travelling Howadji with a bouquet for his table, and the rare visit of their lord, who is as intermittent in his favours as he is to the flower-like beauties of his hareem. And when not owned by a Pasha, they are always the Khedive's. He is the Marquis de Carabas of the valley, and everything worth having he has. But his energy somewhat excuses his tyranny. Side by side with obelisks, one sees with surprise a smoking chimney of some manufactory or sugar-works; and all along the bank, insulting the repose of the place, the telegraph spins its thread, and sends stock quotations of London and Paris even before the indignant faces of Hathor and Amun Ra.

In one Pasha's house we saw the whole establishment; the great chairless room with its divan, and cool whitewashed walls, the bed of iron for protection from vermin, the great quilts of curtains which hung before the windows to give that darkness which dismisses the flies and invites the coolness; and finally, the marbled floored bath-room, in which yet lingered the vaporous heat of baths enjoyed and dead. And in the garden attached to this house, I noticed a young palm, round whose slender stalks nature had woven with folds and plaits a brown covering, so like in colour and texture to the mummy cloths that we instantly thought it must have suggested them. Nature thus always offers the first hint to the artisan, the sculptor, the architect. And the delight of our life here is to be in some degree partaking the old Egyptian life, for while drawing from the sculptured stones their secrets of meaning and beauty, we are hourly able to see in things about us what shaped the Egyptian's thought. Nature hints of all these things to us as it did to him.

We left Karnak, as this journal shows, with only those confused and chaotic sentiments of departed grandeur which our hasty visits to the two sides of the river inevitably furnished. But we have seen the grandest temples of worship that man has made, and we know them to be such. The cathedral at Milan, St. Peter's, and even the lovely Parthenon, paled before the overwhelming sublimity of what. we saw at Thebes.

At Erment, Ruskallah had hopes of sweeping the market and replenishing our stores. His forays are generally successful, and as we advance towards Nubia, our boat is hourly assuming the appearance of Noah's Ark. Brown rams bleat from our sandal with the identical profile the men of old gave to their Amun Ra ; the same sparrows of whom our Lord said so many were sold for a farthing, Ruskallah's gun drops upon our deck by dozens, and delicious are they in pies ; the excited vagabond cocks, knowing that our watches have lost their reckoning, crow from their coops at all hours of day and night. And Erment did not fail him. We took that little walk on the brown river-brink so necessary to do justice to all his provision.

As we floated languidly into the sunset, a noble headland on the right seemed to bar our progress, while on the left a sand-

G

spit was covered with a host of pelicans,
whose breasts shone like silver against the
gold of the twilight. It made a lovely
picture, and I tried for it in a sketch. The
breeze freshened at night, and as the
new moon, which looked like the mystic
boat of Osiris, travelled to light us, we
sped away as long as it lasted.

Esné, Wednesday, 18th.

Early the morning of the 16th we and
the *Clara* were at Esné. This is the
second station for the crew's bread-baking,
and we had the whole day before us for
sight-seeing and rambles. Esné also has
its ancient temple; it is particularly interesting, being built under the Ptolemys
by the Romans. What an influence was
that which kept its hold upon the conquerors of the world and made them servants
of the ideas and forms of Egypt! It is
the deepest buried temple we have seen,
but was cleared of earth by Mohammed
Ali in 1842. The light falls from above

and sideways, and brings out beautifully all the profuse chiselling. Though we know the Romans had iron, and therefore, probably, steel, its execution cannot compare with Egyptian work thousands of years older. But what it misses in clearness of line it makes up for by richness. The capitals of its columns are particularly lovely, being like a Roman fantasia on the old simple theme; great varieties of ornaments are introduced, and, for the first time, amid papyrus bud and lotus, we saw boughs of the palm. Many of the head-dresses of the figures were a kind of network of curls, like that which we saw at Mr. Smith's, worn by Cleopatra. He had a paper impression of her head, which fully satisfied us. The plump full face, the sensual lips, the Greek profile, showed us that it was she. It came from a small room at Karnak, were we vainly tried to see the original, blackened by torches, with the help of three torches and plenty of candles. But it was rather high up, and the sooty surface

refused the light.   The female forms in the
temples, whether of goddess or queen, are
strictly marked through the ancient drapery
with only one budding bosom bared ; they
are slender and graceful, as indeed are
all forms, except one class of priests who,
through a dress looking like undershirt
and drawers, show their rotund proportions.   It is odd how little the eye, drawn
as in full face, is noticeable, and even the
square shoulders of a profile figure we
soon get familiar with.   The legs, in their
absence of calf, are like the Arab legs of
to-day ; the sandals of the kings, on great
occasions, turn up in front, and look like
skates.   Few figures wear cloaks or flowing
drapery, and gauzy tissues are marked by
the limbs seen plainly through them.
There are no sculptured earrings, and
bracelets are not common, but necklaces
like those of to-day abound everywhere.
The wasp—terribly accurate—we see con-
stantly sculptured ; the goose is inimitably
well drawn (as indeed are all birds), and

looks like life, but they are often fantastically and untruly coloured. The falcon has
one wing erect and one depressed, as if it
were hurt. In this Esné temple I noticed
several bats, but very badly cut. How
strange it is that in these later Roman
days the hieroglyphic should be intelli-
gently used, and then so suddenly lost!
But Champollion has been for us the
morning light which made music of this
Memnonian silence. Mariette Bey is his
diligent disciple, and even the erudite
Lepsius could at first sight read them off.
What we are now looking for is the
papyrus MS. which shall give us that
wisdom and that poetry which it was not
the duty of the temples to give amidst the
nomenclature of Kings and Gods.

Esné is the home of the ghawazee. A
range of pillared cafés fringe the river, and
near them are the huts and haunts of the
ghawazee. We saw them standing before
their doors, not at all beautiful, in striped and
gaudy dresses of European calico. One of

them came on board—she was better; she was heavy with gold coins worn on brown breast, and round her neck was a circlet of gold horns, such as might have been worn by the Queen of Sheba. She tried to make a sharp bargain with us for a dance in the evening, and even offered for two pounds what she had demanded five for. But Ruskallah on visiting their houses, and the dancing-hall proposed, found all too mean and dirty to be to us attractive. We shall do better to postpone it all for the spacious and cleanly saloon of our consul at Luxor, who will gladly offer us *une nuit égyptienne*. Eugenio returned late in the evening with his book full of sketches of native dahabeahs, which, with their motley crew, strange and oriental jars and boxes, looked as if they were taking freight for Sinbad the Sailor. Nor was it only then that we thought of him, for all the way from Cairo, at the foot of the limestone declivity, or, more like still, shining huge, round, and white, in the solitude of the plain, stands the tomb of a sheikh; it looks precisely like Sinbad's roc's egg, and reminds us of Vedder's picture, where so well he has painted it. Here these tombs, as we pass away from the more populous places of the Nile towards the savageness of Nubia, are less and less frequent.

But we have been for several days in the country of the sakia and the shadoof. There, in the blazing sun, stands at the shadoof a streaming figure of Florentine bronze, as if doomed to labour in vain for sins he had committed. He is Egypt's image of Tantalus, and too sadly he resembles it. The fertility he furnishes shall pass by his own lips, and he stands silent there, robbed of the wealth he creates. He indeed is silent, but his shadoof and sakia moan for him. Their grief, a creak, heard like a refrain of sorrow amid the joy of the sunshine, laments for him. It is the same cry of burthen and over-work that we hear in the voice of the camel, which at times it strangely resembles.

Thursday, December 17th.

The wind was so light that we did not start until noon, and then, by tracking; little by little, that mysterious freshness which falls out of the sky like an elixir as night approaches, and with it the breeze—the friend of coolness—wrought a change on our somewhat jaded spirits. And the tints of evening, which begin so early, already clothed the abrupt and channeled mountains with their mother-of-pearl hues. The landscape insensibly gains in grandeur as we advance, and the once level and battlemented cliffs now rise at times into mountain peaks, their shadows of tender violet lying like chequer work against the golden brown of their surfaces. And the green, which once only inundated the plain, now as the valley narrows, overflows at times even to the water's edge in malachite brilliancy. It seems to us even lovelier, tenderer, than that of the marvellous plains of Asyoot.

But trees are not very numerous ; for
several days we have been in the country
of the dôm-palm, the unsightly brother of
the princely date-palm. The dôm-palm
struggles up but for a short distance, with
two, or at the most three irregular branches,
and his sharp harsh fans are but a poor
substitute for the grace and dignity of his
more favoured brother. All travellers in
Egypt rave about the palm—all journals
say what they can of his majestic beauty,
so let not our journal neglect this splendid
fringe of the Nile. We pass through their
stately crowds singing hosannas and waving
palm branches in praise of the beautiful
river, and though this tree is almost our
only leafy companion, it suffices, so various
is it in charm, through the day's different
hours, or when standing sentinel through
the starry night. And its colours vary as
do the colours of everything here through
the nice gradations of daylight, and through
brightness and shadow. As the fresh
morning strikes it, it is often of a silvery-

green, sometimes sparkling as though Damascus blades were there inlaid with gems, and in full light its stem is a golden brown, warmer than any other tints in the landscape. It is serrated at its edges, and when, with mighty spring, it launches itself against the sky, it often looks like a rocket which bursts in flakes of green radiance. And when the wind is strong, its graceful hair is tossed over its eyes, all streaming the same way, and we then talk of the "procession of the palms," as at home we have talked of the procession of the pines. Twilight, and such a twilight as ours, is its hour of greatest beauty, for then it borrows magic and mystery from the night, and evening slowly dies behind its dusky pillars in a glow of sombre orange, while its lofty crest towers one solid mass of shadow in startling relief from the fading brightness. We have called the palm princely and regal, and well may England's prince acknowledge this, whose crest has the same lines of beauty, and whose legend, *Ich dien* (I serve), humbly proud, might well be that of this benefactor of mankind.

We had had clouds all day—a thing so rare here as to please by its variety. In the morning I had noticed an unusually heavy dew, which must have supplied the moisture. We anticipated the tumultuous discord of its beauty as the sun set, but all was serene as usual, only the floor of heaven was " paved with patines of bright gold " instead of the graduated hyacinth of cloudless days. But a surprise awaited us. We were to enjoy our first Egyptian moon, for the thin circlet of the first two nights which so captivated the Turk that he made it

> " A peaceful symbol in a warlike banner
> On Yemen's happy hills ; "

and last night's level curves, the boat of Osiris, had given way to a moon sufficiently full to make for us a night such as we had not known before. Long did we linger on our divans, enjoying the faultless atmosphere, ourselves, and every indented gorge of the hills about us, flooded with its silent influence.

On the softly bleak and arid eminences we could fancy we saw the jackal which Ruskallah promises us, and indeed anywhere here a sheep tied to a stake could give lively hopes to the expectant sportsman.

The breeze blew merrily and cool, and existence was but another word for happiness. Only consideration for the Arabs, who make our airy saloon their sleeping place, took us below, and soon the music of our prow mixed itself with dreams of home and remembrances of a world so unlike this.

Friday, December 18th.

At dawn I drew my curtain, and saw, just facing my window, the gigantic propylon of a temple which I knew must be Edfoo.

As we must not pass everything going up the river, we treated ourselves to a visit to the temple here. It was within a quarter of an hour's easy donkey trot, and we arrived with that freshness, without which such thoughtful sightseeing is a losing battle, before the temple's massive entrance.

From afar the prodigious walls, covered with gigantic figures, were clearly outlined in the morning's light, and insatiate of sketching, I instantly fell to work, and Eugenio sent for the box which he had neglected to bring; but when brought he did nothing. He could only sit with folded hands, saturating himself with such fulness of beauty as a half-hour's sketching must render imperfectly. For this is in some sense the gem of Egypt. It is a perfect temple within and without, and we saluted with honour Mariette Bey, the present conservator of antiquities, who had so recently rescued this beauty from the huts and dirt which disfigured and hid it.

It is not the business of this journal to
give measurements, outlines, or records of
the past.   Has not Murray his seven
columns upon it ? and does it not shine in
Wilkinson and Lepsius ?   We can give
only impressions, and those flying ones,
and as those are always of the same
beauty and grandeur, words fail us in
recurrent monotony of delight.   Besides the
completeness, we had a sense of elegance
in the proportions of the courts and
columns, which we afterwards found explained when we remembered it was
Europe's grace added to that of Egypt.
For like the temple at Esné this is Ptolemaic, and has the same lightness, which
the severer architecture of old refuses.   It
is recovered from the earth as is Pompeii,
and would be perfect throughout but for
the ruthless hand of the iconoclast.   Here,
as everywhere, the faces of kings and gods
are hewn away.   We fear that the same
Coptic Christian hand which elsewhere
has defaced the loveliness Greece and

Rome left in our charge, has been at its merciless work. This temple is so undisturbed, except by such defacement, that in the inner sanctuary is yet its Holy of Holies. There is a tablet where it is said was placed the figure of the god—the Hawk-headed deity of Egypt—Hor-hat, as Murray says, or according to Lepsius, Hathor. We looked at it with deep reverence as being perhaps the germ of the Jewish tabernacle. The beautifully proportioned columns of the first court have florid capitals. They all differ from each other in luxuriant variety of design, and here again, as at Esné, we saw the palm bough which the old Egyptians neglected. Indeed one capital was composed entirely of these—the whole bough down to its insertion in the trunk. And the fern was elsewhere delicately cut, and other plants. These capitals were of the Corinthian order of Egypt as compared to the simpler lotus and papyrus-bud epoch. In one corridor we saw what we did not

understand—a chain of figures, each alternate one masculine, but with an old
female's pendent breast.   In the corridor
that corresponded on the other side was
a strange series of sculptured pictures of
aquatic sports.   Here was the old boat
for fishing, very like an Indian canoe, and
its sails elaborately reticulated, as if bamboo over papyrus cloth, were always square.
The long lateen sail, now the only one,
was then wholly unknown; and in these
boats were sportsmen, women being among
them, who harpooned the hippopotamus
precisely as we now harpoon the whale,
for a running rope was fastened to their
spear.   The hippopotami were all repre-
sented very little—its size being incon-
venient—and the sportsmen, like the
triumphing king, made more gigantic than
his victims.   The sail of this boat had a
yard at the top, which seemed to turn on a
pivot like the Nile boats now.   The ropes
were all indicated, but I suppose this to
have been a boat of the smaller class.

Some of the old stairs of the temple remain, and we ascended and stood upon
the huge slabs of the roof, which was then
only the first story, as ascending, broken
stairs showed. The view thence was a
new one to us. We saw our dear Nile
as a distant object, flowing pearl-like between its emerald banks like the river of
a dream.

We were back at the boat and off by
noon. Again a feeble wind which, as
before, strengthened with the strengthen-
ing coolness, and forbade our stopping,
carried us well through the night. Towards evening the flocks were on the
wing, and one mighty one in our wake
drifted to and fro, like smoke or clouds of
autumn leaves. We hoped they were wild
geese; they came steadily on, unfurling
their lines and whirling in their mysterious
eddies directly over our heads—then we
could see by the familiar shape that they
were pelicans. There must have been
five hundred of them. Ruskallah and I

H

fired both our barrels without effect, for the pelican is impenetrable except by the bullet.

Night deepened, and at last the moon rose, and as her silvery radiance flooded everything, and blanched the stars, we heard from the ghostly cliffs upon our left the cry of the jackal we had waited for. And a little farther on, from the other side, in strange contrast to it, came the shouts and laughter of Arab children at play.

Though the moon was our friend and the wind too, our night was not comfortable. We do not mind shipwreck much on the Nile. In fact we are wrecked at least once every day, and if we sail then, by night also. We well know the slow slip of the boat, which after a tremor comes to a stand-still, but at night it is less pleasant—for when we feel our bed lift as if some crocodile were suddenly under us, and soon hear the sailors' wild cry as with their long red poles they push us afloat, we are disturbed and angry — not to mention the villanous creak of the rudder, which sounds like a sakia in distress. But soon, as the boat drops into the quiet of its natural bed, we with it drop again into slumber.

I drew the curtain at dawn, remembering the surprise of yesterday's ruin, and lo! here was another. Rising from an eminence, and just over the water, towered the broken propylon and half-buried columns of a temple—it could be none other than Kom Ombos. Mounted on its picturesque acclivity, with a soft morning light upon it, we thought it the most beautiful thing we had yet seen. Even at the distance we were, every lotus curve and floating shadow was pencilled as clearly as the forms of a flower which the hand holds. We all cried out, Stop! but the wind and Ruskallah were inexorable, and so we stood and watched it fading—fading, but definite and lovely to the last—till Paolo rang the bell for breakfast.

Saturday, 19th.

Our wind held gloriously; when it is light the *Clara* holds her own with us, but to-day we again ran away from her.   Before long we were surprised by the colour of the sand, which swept down from crags to the plain a broad sheet of glowing gold. The river sand-bars look cold and steely beside it.   Ah! this then is at last Africa, and we are near the watery portal of her cataracts; for Egypt, peopled so long ago by some wandering Caucasian tribe who found life there sweeter than their nomadic one, had neither by its origin nor by its long relations with Judea, Greece, and Rome, ever been really African.   Had she so been we had not borrowed from her most of what we know.   But here was Africa. The hills were emphasised with rocks, fatigued and weary-looking with long life, knobby and dark with strange resemblances to the heads of negroes, as they surrounded us; and at last started up, phantom-like, even from the river. Yes; at last we saw solid rocks in that river's bed which till now had been soft as down. A little turn in the river and we had a glimpse of the island of Elephantine and the few minarets belonging to Assouan.

We saw in the distance a fellow-traveller, an English boat, and early in the afternoon were fairly lodged beside her. Again Africa instantly proclaimed itself as we indolently waited for the coming coolness to go on shore. The beach soon swarmed with blacks, tributaries as they looked, merchants really, offering to us Africa and its golden joys. There were men and girls holding up for purchase Nubia's pretty bracelets and anklets, its abbreviated female costume made of braided leather strips, baskets which, in the distance, looked like the pottery of Cyprus in their form and colours, and great handsful of ostrich feathers, which fluttered in the wind. A slave-trader, with endlessly long gun, looked like a reproduction from " Uncle

Tom's Cabin," none the less that he wore the broad white trousers of the planter. There were men with ebony staffs, and girls with Nubian necklaces, and later they brought a huge stuffed hyena and planted it over against us.

After a little ramble through the town and skirmishing among the shops, we returned to enjoy the evening at Elephantine. As our sandal touched the shore we were waited upon by a dusky cloud of male and female urchins, each holding up something to sell. These Nubian children differ from Arab ones in being always ready for a scare. If you look steadily at them they wither away and fly, and when the gentle Abdallah waved his gigantic staff, they scampered away like a flock of frightened birds, but always to come back again. There was that magnet in our pockets before which their terrors were vain. And so in a cloud they kept with us till we reached the crest of the island, where, amid the crumbling masonry of brick, after noticing a solitary pathetic Egyptian god of granite and a mined gateway, we looked far down the Nile of our future. There was something terrible in the scene. The rocks did not look like those of earth as we knew them——they might have belonged to another planet; and some had the impossible grotesque aspect of stage rocks in some opera. The river, indented and islanded with these strange masses, reminded me of Lake Winapissiogge. Like, but how different. On our return the usual whispers were circulating of a delay; some ill-behaved rocks were badly placed for us at the present height of the river. It was delightful to thus overtake these playful stories in our books of Nubian fashions.

Sunday, 20th.

We have plenty of leisure, and while the ladies reposed from the fatigue of two nights of sailing, Eugenio and I donkeyed off to the quarries. On the way we came to a large square tomb, bearing the following inscription :—

" In memory of Daniel Cave * of Clave Hill, Glostershire. Drowned at the Cataracts. Age 25."

The " Clave " is probably a misprint. It wasn't a pleasant sight to people on their way to the same danger, and there was something terribly pathetic in this solitude of an English grave. Not far from it was a little Nubian cemetery. Ever since Asyoot the houses have been more and more Egyptian ; their inclined line exactly conforming to that of a temple's propylon. And these little graves looked like miniature pyramids of Dashoor. But the quarry of syenite—the Egyptian granite which Rome coveted so much, and of which to-day the museums of the Vatican and the Louvre are so full ! Being there was indeed being behind the scenes. The whole crest of the hill had been worked,

* Drowned, we were told, in attempting to go down the Cataract on a log like the Nubians.

and carried off; an infinity of blocks
strewed the plain, and some sublime
towering masses caught Eugenio's eye,
and he found room for their grand lines
in his sketch-book. Like the quarry at
Pentelicus, this one seemed but abandoned
yesterday. Here, everywhere were the
marks of that famous chisel which the
learned would have us believe was made
of hardened bronze. Yet we know of no
such hardened bronze, and steel must have
been there; it is only fair in Egypt to
suppose the men of old knew everything,
had everything they desired, till we dis-
cover the contrary.

Little marks in a close line showed
where the wedges of wood, expanded by
water, sufficed to split enormous blocks.
But we were fairly posed when we came
upon a gigantic obelisk, whose length we
could only guess, as each end is buried;
but its breadth, by measurement, we found
to be more than eleven feet; it was but
rough hewn—unpolished, and but for what

we know of these artists of old, we might have supposed it like Robinson Crusoe's boat, left there because it could not be got to the water.

But we know they moved such masses all over Egypt as if they were chips of wood, though we only dimly surmise how they did it. Such a mass would sink any raft that ever floated, and yet they *were* floated on rafts ; and when its destination was reached, no mechanics, seemingly, could elevate them—but they *did* elevate them, and no doubt in a way as simple as it was ingenious, though one day all Paris stood open-mouthed to see its cleverest men re-enact what Luxor had already done half-a-dozen times.

Returning, we noticed the young wheat growing in those raised squares like garden-beds, the whole so comically like in form our beloved waffles. Immediately on our return, imposing persons were seen moving along the shore and entering our dahabeah. They were the famous reis captains of the Cataract, and had not cared to move till now. A solemn council was held, at which Ruskallah presided. The reis and dragoman of the *Clara* shared in the council. It was almost certain that that incredibly naughty rock must delay us; but after pipes and coffee, and the luxury of procrastination, Ruskallah announced to our joy that if the wind were favourable to-morrow we go up.

The secretary of Sir Samuel Baker, who now deigns to be a merchant, and at whose ivory teeth and tropic smile of sweetness I looked with deep respect, as belonging to Khartoun—an Africa beyond our hopes —brought for us a cloud of ostrich feathers. We fondled and caressed them, and finally dared make our purchases. The ladies secured these treasures beloved of women, and I purchased for far away dear ones two long exquisite feathers of white, at a Napoleon each, which Queen Titania might have deigned to wear.

There is a look of desolatian and sadness about Syene (Assouan now, and thus changed by Coptic and Arab alteration) which makes it a most suitable place for the victim of a tyrant.

Here Juvenal lingered in exile till death. How often must he have sat dejected and indignant upon the rocks before our eyes.

JUVENAL AT SYENE.

Here at the utmost bound of Roman power,
Thy prison walls the Arabian—Lybian waste,
Slave over slaves, thy tyrant bade thee cower,
Even by the soldier's office more disgraced,
Eating thy indignant heart out through each hour,
And every drop of Exile's chalice taste.
   Take comfort, noble heart, for while the hand
Which held thee loosens in the charnel's dust,
That shameless forehead bears its eternal brand,
Yet in thy living page, and cruelty's lust,
Cut into deathless adamant shall stand,
So that Oblivion spare its pitying rust,
But thy name, brightening through these Christian
   years,
Virtue shall speak it but with grateful tears.

How often have we not watched at

evening the lonely stork musing among the shallows.

Here there are no shallows ; all is frowning and demoniac rock. Our journal for a time takes farewell of this bird in these lines :——

THE STORK IN EGYPT.

Dark against light, as sculptured by the hand,
Reverent of life in days which are no more,
Silent, immovable, I see thee stand
Upon the golden burnish of the shore.

Thy life is of to-day, but since the wave
That mirrors thee has flowed from Afric's heart,
Immortal in the lines which rob the grave,
One of a worshipped host thou wert a part.

Rememberest thou the regal fanes afar,
Where sleeps the long procession of thy race,
And, balmed in consecrated slumber, are
High-chambered in each sacred dwelling-place ?

Or, as in dream, far in the frozen North,
Seest thou thy boreal nest with ice-hung eaves,
And to the spicy South, in venturing forth,
Knowest that regret which Home behind us leaves ?

I hail thee, brother of those austere skies,
Among the untravelled creatures of the sun,
And I salute with fortunate surprise
The fellowship which makes our being one.

Dream on, and I with thee would dream of those
Whose love can still remember thee and me,
Till our thought, borne past yonder fields of rose,
Shares the same flight above the severing sea.

IN SIGHT OF THE CATARACT.

Monday, 21st.

In Nubia a boat is a travelling farm, with not only the poultry-yard, but sheep, and, perhaps, if we had room for them, buffaloes, so needful to us is their milk. The camel is a picturesque, incredible creature, but the buffalo is impossible. It seems a brother of the cave-bear, the megatherium, and other queer creatures, which were Nature's rough sketches for the animals we know now. He is ill-drawn throughout, and his slaty-grey is a colour no cattle should have; his eye is bloodshot and glassy, and has a pleading mournful look, as if sad for the survival of his fellows. Uncanny as he is, the cow's milk is rich and sweet. It is the most peaceful of animals. I fear we shall see few in Nubia, and nothing can we miss more. Our fellow-passengers—the chickens, turkeys, and sheep—it is delightful to see their enjoyment when liberated from coop and boat for the shore. The fowls shake out their feathers, make up their quarrels, and strut about with the air of Howadjis on their travels. Our three sheep, with lesser liberty, tied to a post, instantly fall to on halfa grass and beans, fattening for they know not what. There is cannibalism in the thought of thus eating our fellow-voyagers, and when shipwrecked in mid river we recall with a shudder the tales of sailors eating each other. Of our three sheep one is very pretty, with spots of black and white; one a golden brown, as if cut out of syenite, and with a huge tuft on his head, and the largest of Ethiopian blackness, and the profile of Jupiter Ammon.

They all have that strange caudal plumpness for which South Africa in its way is so famous.

Chickens are small and pretty, and delightful eating—the turkeys, and they all seem turkey poults—rank next to American ones for excellence. Turkeys and chickens are our chief dependence on the Nile; other meats may fail us, but these never, and Antonio is always astonishing us with fresh variations on this theme.

I am interrupted by a cry from Ruskallah. The reis has hooked a mighty fish, and his shape is described and his merits discounted before he is seen. An Arab stands ready with his gaff, but, alas! he slips away at the surface, and, Ruskallah's bulk interposing, I don't see him.

Of course we are not to go up the cataract to-day; there is not wind enough—there never is. We now know the sun of Nubia. Its stab is direct and searching, so we sit under an awning and watch the yellow sand-hills wrapping us like a lion's tawny

hide all around, and the black, astonishing
rocks of syenite, which we thought basalt
till we met one with its top knocked off.
We see afar a line of foam, and hear a
gentle roar, which, we presume, is the
terrible cataract ; and we watch our Nubians
going home for the night across the lustrous
river on palm-tree logs, their feet along
the log, and their hands towing and sup-
porting them at the same time. We took
a little walk, and, before I found it out, I
had eaten the fruit of the castor-oil, seeing
a native do it, and found it not bad. This
land is the paradise of apothecaries ; castor-
oil flows as in his dreams, and everywhere
he has the smell of his shop. He would
be pleased with the look of the rocks here :
they would so remind him of knobby
chunks of liquorice ; and the cantharides of
Spain must yield to the pungency of the
Nubian fly.

The change everything has undergone
since entering Nubia is miraculous. It is
greater than the change from England to

I

France, though the water here unites, not
divides, and the narrow gate which we
have passed through entering Nubia to-
day seemed to shut it from Egypt. The
Nile had not a fifth of its usual width;
many rocks were sculptured to the water's
edge with hieroglyphics; everything looked
formidable and fascinating. High on the
right everywhere the beautiful sand of gold,
like mountains of gold dust; it looked as if
it had been running through Time's outstretched hand since Creation's dawn. It
is of the same colour as the sand in Mr.
Longfellow's little hour-glass, on which he
wrote these lines we so much delight to
remember here. Though that sand was
red, as it is here, it came from the Holy
Land. Night gave it a new beauty, under
the full moon it retained its colour, and had
the flush of snow seen by the reflection
of a great fire; and long and steadily
did we look at it then, for a party was
organised between our two dahabeahs
to scale the sandy height and see what

the desert beyond held.   Ruskallah with
pistols and lantern went also.   In the clear
moonlight we could see the figures toiling
along, as through the glass I have seen
climbers relieved against the snow of
Mont Blanc.   And the lantern danced
along fantastically, now precipitate and
now delayed, suggesting guesses as to the
cause of it.   At last they were upon the
crest, their figures relieved against the sky.
Ruskallah fired repeated shots, which we
heard, but handkerchiefs were waved which
we could not see.   Then all disappeared.
At length the lantern tumbled down the
slope, and we could see the party pause as
if weary.   After their return, they told us
the delay was caused by the crumbling
rocks falling about them.   They had gone
inland, ascending a high point, whence
their sight for the first time embraced a
wide sweep of real desert.   Sand in
billows as far as the horizon, with black
rocks like islands.   The party were enchanted with their excursion, and found

the fresher air of the hill-top far superior
to ours below. And yet it seemed to us
perfection as we lay upon our divans. So
dry is this elastic night air that we lay an
hour with our hats off with no fear of
colds, and yet our London letters speak
of bitter weather, snow and ice, and all
those miracles of climate which would be
as strange to the Arab as are these tropic
wonders to us. It seemed a shame to go
below, and to leave to neglect and waste
such a moonlight as only Nubia knows.
This night, so softly bright, has not the
harsh splendour of ours ; its shadows, its
outlines, are more delicate ; and the heavens
both by day and night, seem nearer to us
than ours. The lights, the shadows, are
infinitely soft and tender. Indeed softness
is about us everywhere in Egypt. It is in
the gentle, gracious speech of the Arab ;
the water is the softest of water, and the
soft earth moulds our feet as we move.
The naked footprints of the Arabs, deep in
the mud, harden as the sun dries, and it

divides into great cakes like our spring
ice. And these hardened footprints always
remind me of the only thing that we have
which can proudly challenge Egypt in
antiquity—the fossil footprints of the Connecticut Valley. And the mud must have
been much the same as this. Like this,
it was compacted and triturated by the
drain of a continent. The Connecticut
Valley must have been like the Nile in
overflow, and its inhabitants were mostly
aquatic. The gigantic bird footprints are
now considered to be reptilian, and we
have here already seen huge lizards, which
the natives call the sons of crocodiles, and
one of which Ruskallah shot, but it turned
over and disappeared into the water.

At Assouan we saw a man whose
profession it is to shoot crocodiles for
travellers. For that purpose he goes with
them for so much money in their dahabeahs.

Tuesday, December 22d.

Not only no signs of ascending the Cataract, but the smart wind from the east is most unfavourable. It is also most disagreeable. The pains and pleasures of Egypt are both keen. The scale is exquisite, and one swiftly passes from rapture to despair. The same day will contain the sullen oppressive heat of noon and the bliss of evening, which seems then an euthanasia. This wind was the formidable Kemseen—the wind that sometimes buries a caravan in the desert. The fine sand flies past our boat and makes life above stairs impossible. But it by no means is Kemseen at its worst, for Ruskallah, in defiance of it, has, with Sapienza, slipped down the river to Assouan, in hopes of our much desired paint and beer, and with some prospect of letters. Alas! they returned without them, but fortunately the *Clara* can lend me the " Times " which it receives. How strangely does this journal read here among our naked Nubians. In this simple savage life it pictures to us our complicated civilisation—like an intricate tracery of frostwork, which, though possible in England, would at once dissolve in the sun of Africa. And how painful to read of the English Premier kissing the dust in apology before a wave of the gauntleted hand of Bismarck. It has a touch of that oriental submissiveness which we should only look for in the earliest annals of his race. And the political letters from America, how in them we hear the stir and hum of our political wasps, and let us hope also, not without the honest buzz of the true honey-bees of our busy hive.

The present success of the Democratic party is a reaction—a new swing of the national pendulum, without which our clockwork might come to confusion, or run down and stand still. Some one has said that our national life is chronic revolution—the nation is always being saved—and it is true that the people's life is expressed by these swift movements of the rudder, without which it might go on the rocks, as may we yet in our deferred ascent of the Cataract.

But that this is a crisis of real meaning in our affairs is too plainly evident, for what does Democracy stand for, hatched as it was in the scheming brain of that most French of Americans, and truest of Virginians, Thomas Jefferson?

Its meaning thus far has been a party sustained and led at the North in the interests of slavery. Can it have its old meaning now that that service is dead and buried for ever? It had the air of being not only American, but the true expression of the honest popular will; but at heart it was more Russian than American. For the Southerner never was an American. Whether he would or no he was the slave of the slave, and drank from his peculiar institution that which is poison to American freedom. Perhaps the absence of liberty of opinion, in no time and in no country, was ever so striking as in Southern free America on the slavery question.

The bait the slave-owner threw to his Northern servant—and I have seen him years ago express to one of his tools, through the studied courtesy then necessary, his loathing and contempt for the abjectness so useful to him—the bait he threw to the North was *office*, and from the hungry wolves went up the cry "To the victors belong the spoils!"

Now that the national spectre is laid, it would seem that we must hereafter sleep in peace. If we typify the struggle of our parties by names that have had force here, and speak of Osiris and Typho—all Typho can scare us with now is repudiation. Every Jeremy Diddler of the nation would find his democracy in that. But a nation of business men knows that repudiation is bankruptcy. Republicanism, as a war party in peace, must of itself soon cease, and good men must hope that the future victories of Democracy may be really American ; that it shall mean, not America's death, but the life of America.

Wednesday, 23d.

Last evening, and the evening before, our sailors occupied their enforced idleness under the moon in sportive games. The sand at last comes down and touches our boat. The lion has conquered the lamb. As we penetrate Africa, thinner grows the strip of cultivation, till, from the sheeted plains of verdure round Cairo, it diminishes to a slender ribbon, and here is limited to now and then a patch of emerald shining in the gold-setting of the desert sand. Yes, the desert has conquered, and we have come here to see its victory. Wherever wheat waves there is a look of sweetness and humanity. That is gone. And on these calcined rocks desolation sits like an Ethiop queen.

Our Arabs seem cultivated citizens compared with man's savageness here. It was delightful to see them on the moonlit sandbank, playing their games. They danced to and fro in its beams with spectral agility. They played at single-stick with their long staffs, and they played at cloche-pied, till they fell into the delicious sand. Leap-frog followed, and over all merrily rang an incessant peal of childish laughter. And how happy and childlike was their fun, so easily obtained and so thorough! One could not think but with pain how Boston's mayor and council tried on the Fourth of July to purchase the mournful smile with which the crowded hillside of the Common rewards them. Not to be outdone, we withdrew to a privacy of moonlight, took off our shoes and stockings, and buried our feet in the sand, to know what Memnon feels. It was delicious. This fine matrix, cool on the surface from the night, was warmer and warmer as we penetrated it. We half-buried each other, and played that we were masterpieces of ancient art which somebody was finding. Magnetism from the earth stole so pleasantly to our limbs that we could have stayed there for ever, and while we lingered we planned such a night in the desert, double-tented with the *Clara* people, and so to drink deeper from the magic cup of the desert, our tiny drop of which was to us so pleasant.

There is a hum about us of movement and cries. Can it be that the impassive sheikhs mean business? We had begun to feel enchanted like some shadak in search of the waters of oblivion, and that here we should live and die, hearing for ever the musical mockery of the Cataract.

Thursday, Dec. 24th.

The enchantment continues. To be sure we have moved, and had a taste of the Cataract. The grizzled chieftain of the waters and his swarm of followers decided at least to change our prison, and it was very good fun while it lasted. The Cataract has seven "gates" as they are called—locks, as it were—and we have passed two. These two and the final gate are the only ones of serious difficulty. It was all just as we have read in the books, and we cannot pretend to a catastrophe which did not occur. The men in our sandal passed a long rope round one of the knobby rocks, or pulled in a file of about forty, while their sheikh superintended. The Arabic flew about like a sandstorm, and I could excuse Fenimore Cooper's bad joke in one of his novels, where the scene is laid in Africa, and an American captain insists on calling the head man "a shriek." But Cooper certainly was not strong in joking, unless he considered his prudish and solemn young ladies a kind of fun.

At the worst points, the compacted Nile spread in glassy blisters like boiling oil, and the strain on the men then was severe. There was the excitement of a possible failure, and the *Rachel* hung for a while slewing upon the rocks. Fenders were put out; our sailors, including the reis, using their bodies as fenders even, and finally, amid a thousand wild cries, she slipped into the polished pool above. There we lay while the heavier *Clara* was to be pulled through. This accomplished we were easily dragged along a bit farther, and lodged early in the afternoon against the left bank. We have had ample time since to feel the cruel delay where time is so precious. But we have fished, and shot, and walked, and climbed. The rocks of this country are unaccountable. These syenite boulders are built up by some hand into gigantic cairns, usually surmounted by the largest of them all. And these are scattered as far as the eye can reach. It is weird and wild, and seems a part of the spell by which some magician has enchanted us. Towards evening we climbed one of these cairns, enjoying the strange scene, where the Nile was a chequer-work of gold among the forty sable islands which I counted. We saw Philæ hanging there in the twilight like some Promised Land, which we were only to see from afar, and then, like Moses, perish upon our little Pisgah of the Cataract.

The weather was troubled and warm. Gauzy clouds were drawn across the sky, and when at last the full moon, with veiled radiance, rose above one of these grotesque cairns, all was strangely picturesque. The top stone here, very human as they often are, looked, too, like some enchanted prince turned to stone.

There are tufts of long grass growing in the river. Their vivid green illuminates the duskiness of the rocks. Here and there a solitary palm grows, and a low, humble village is behind them, meaner and more forlorn than those of Lower Egypt ever are. The Nubians who inhabit them are the most venerable of peoples. Their language is said to be derived from that of old Egypt, and their savage ways have not changed for thousands of years. Spears with steel points and oblong shields of rhinoceros's hide, with a knob in the centre, like that of the Highlanders, are offered us for sale; also quivers full of arrows, and massive silver bracelets, which have been the fashion in Queen Candace's day; and gourds, with painted patterns like the earliest pottery, are brought to us. And daggers—for every Nubian wears a dagger slipped under a leathern bracelet on his left arm—and long necklaces of shells, and the costume *au grand complet* which is held up, while the vendor laughs, and cries, " Madame Nubia !"

The Nubian sailors, we are told, are quick in quarrel, and cannot bear a word. They blaze up in a moment with the unchecked flow of savage emotion, and the Khedive as yet has not managed to make them submit to any fashion but their own as to the Cataract ascent. They receive their full pay at once, and work when they will. They come over late in the morning, and go home early in the evening on the little logs of wood, where they balance themselves so cleverly, keeping their clothes dry on the tops of their heads. A Nubian

OUR NUBIAN PILOT.

showed me one of these logs which was hollow, offering little friction, and not two feet long; but for swimming it is placed under the breast, while upon the larger logs the men sit upright. In the evening they dot the river everywhere, and animate a scene otherwise so desolate.

The Nubian is fierce, but also, certainly, when young, full of fun. I had a school of some twenty boys who repeated our English numerals after me, thus returning Arabia's original gift to us. The rogues seemed to learn readily, shouting each number in unison pretty accurately. I promised any who was perfect up to ten, a piastre. They immediately won plenty, when it turned out that they have known them all a long time, practising from year to year. And as they recited they all showed their teeth, which are much larger, the two front ones especially, than are the handsomer teeth of the Arabs. Their heads are all shaven close, and shine when they swim like footballs among the eddies.

K

When they emerge from the water their skin is studded with diamonds ; it has, too, a most agreeable feel, reminding one of satin.   In our animal economy, when a draught causes a need of supply, nature rushes to the rescue.   Already of old the Greeks had noticed the thickness of skull of the old Egyptians, and we are familiar with the fact as shown in the skull of the American negro.   White boys fighting black boys were always told "to kick him on the shin, to make his nose bleed," the skull not minding raps.   These Nubians affront the steep sun of mid-day with only a thin skull-cap, or mostly nothing at all. Their only turban as headgear, and then it is enormous, is when they cross the river with their clothes upon their heads.

Christmas.

Was there ever such a Christmas in so strange a place ! It is the intensest of African days, and the thermometer stood in our cabin, at 3 P.M., at ninety-three

Fahrenheit. And it was really hard work for the small gang of men at the rope, the Cataract captain had left, the government, just now, having taken most of them. The scene at its short crisis had a dramatic interest as the boat hung balanced on the Cataract. It receded and advanced, whilst a sheikh with his wand shouted and danced like mad to encourage his men, and the gods above looked down upon this Homeric contest of untamed nature with the trained forces of barbarism. But why enlarge upon the details of our ascent, which we find identical with all travellers' descriptions ? It is the opera of the Cataract, with the same leading actors, the same episodes of the double chorus of men, wailing as they pull, and boys, as they slide through the rushing water, singing their chorus of "backsheesh!" which they have practised so long and so well. It was the same as ever, even in the details ; the same snapping of an oar—the same throwing of dust upon his head by the

despondent sheikh—and the same need of
rum and brandy to revive the failing forces
of the captain of the Cataract. And
fortunately we hope the same happy dé-
nouement after our toil, of tranquil rest at
Philæ—but not for to-day. Christmas
was well kept by the Nubians, who after
getting us through a couple of gates more,
left us in the sun, and retired to the shady
rocks to give themselves up to religious
contemplation. As soon as the sun re-
lented, Eugenio and I retired to bathe in
a pool, beside the plunging water. It was
indeed delicious. The water was as cool
as we could wish, and drew from us something of the heat and the fret of these
hideous Nubian delays. The neriads of
the stream, in the shape of a dozen tiny
blackamoors, danced and swam around us.
They also volunteered their acquaintance
with our numerals, and admired, while we
dressed, the complications of braces and
waistcoat. Before long we reposed, re-
freshed, in the shadow of a great rock—

the demoniac scenery all round us, and our impish urchins trying to win our pocket-money by a fantasia—a most comic caricature of the dancing of the gawhazee; so debauched is the infant mind of African simplicity already. Rousseau would hardly have recognised the savage of his dreams.

In the evening we dined with the people of the *Clara*, as they had kindly invited us to make a common Christmas dinner, and we were glad to give a half-holiday to our indefatigable cook—who had presented us at lunch with a cake of frosted sugar, towering like a sheikh's tomb from the dish, whence depended twin banners, with the stars and stripes—and also to Paolo, that perfect servant, without whom life would be impossible. Mr. Porcher had visited us previous to the dinner to inquire if we meant to come in full dress, when I told him that I had thoughts of putting on my stockings, which I thought going very far in Africa.

What a terrible thing it is to be an

Englishman. He must carry England in little with him wherever he goes. He cannot escape. England expects every man to do his duty, and that duty consists in this :——To split his hair up behind with a couple of brushes ; to have by him his india-rubber bath-tub, even though the Nile flow at his foot; to believe in "Murray" and the "English Book of Common Prayer" as sufficient gospel for the Hawadji everywhere ; to carry the feelings, habits, and prejudices of the temperate zone to the equator, and to consider the natives of the countries he passes through as merely "foreigners." These must be terrible conditions of existence to him.

We found a generous hospitality on the *Clara*, for there is artistic rivalry between cuisines of consort dahabeahs. And above all, it was not a little thing for us of two great and friendly nations in this far land to have a common interest in a day that means so little to that very East, once the scene of this unspeakable event.

We felt a bond which held us, though our national lives are so different. The American idea seems really more unintelligible to the English than it would be to an Arab. They are under a necessity of reading us backwards. The devotion of a country's youth to its salvation, inconceivable, perhaps, when the spirit of gain is devouring a nation's honour, must be read off as "fratricidal contest." The exultation and swiftness of national life, which an American proclaims as frankly as he feels it, jealousy must describe as "bumptiousness" and "brag." The Arcadian simplicity of young people, which the duenna and the gouvernante have not yet overtaken, is counted as "wildness." And yet England's inability to do justice to the American idea keeps the nations wholesomely apart. There is with us enough sentimental reverence for the home of our fathers—enough affection for England's literature and greatness to make America feel truly her child. But it is best there should be no half-sympathies, no poor affectation of regard between systems so radically different.   In England the governing class is called the nobility; in America it is called the people.   In England every one tries to overtake and imitate those above him; in America no prosperity, no political success, will separate a man from his fellows.   The atmosphere around aristocracy is repulsion; each avoids the other as possibly not his peer; the atmosphere round the people is attraction—common manhood and common difficulties make them one. The result is, in the one case, sympathy, broadening daily through every avenue of life; and, in the other case, a mild disdain, which first separates Englishmen from Englishmen, and then England from all the nations of the world.

Dec. 26th, Saturday.

A cooler day, and fortunate that it was so, for in yesterday's heat we could not

have borne our disappointment and anger
at seeing close by us the peaceful pool
above the last gate, and we again delayed
from Philæ and repose by these intoler-
able sheikhs. They are as impracticable
as the forces of nature ; and, as the wind
bloweth where it listeth, so these men
come and go at their own sweet will. We
have coddled and placated the chief of the
Cataract as might a Nubian his idol—we
have saluted him in good English—have
cried " Tayeb !" when we thought it was
not " tayeb " at all ; and finally have tried
to melt his soul with full draughts of rum
and brandy. Not a bit of it! the day is
over at 2 P.M., and there is only about
twenty or thirty yards to go. So may
have Prometheus, on some hot Caucasian
crag, have shifted his agonised limbs upon
the rock waiting for a delivery which
seemed never to come. But while we
devote the sheikh and his followers to the
infernal gods, let us admit that the pull
to-day was the stiffest we have had, and

perhaps the lumbering *Clara* did really finish the little strength our lighter *Rachel* may have left.   At any rate we must cry " Kesmet ! " it is fate, and smoke the pipe of resignation.

Sunday, 27th.

The dreadful secret is now out.   We have long seen it in each other's faces, and timidly whispered it to Ruskallah, but now there can be no disguise as to the fatal cause of our delay.   It is the dervish Sheikh Selim—he must be the cause of it in punishment for not visiting him at How as we should.   This dervish is the pride and terror of the country round.   He sits still, and all come to him.   Travellers commonly visit him and give alms, which he instantly divides with the poor.   When travellers go by without a visit he sends his jettatura after them, and stops their boats.   So it must have been with us. The belief in the evil eye—eyn hassondé —is universal on the Nile.   Our sailors attribute everything to it. When the fishing is bad by perfume they neutralise the evil influence. They stick a knife in the mast to avoid it, and it certainly is interesting to find Egypt preceding Italy in this as in most of her beliefs, if indeed we must not go even to Asia for its origin. We see on the figures in the temples a square amulet hung around the neck, just like what the Neapolitan fishermen of to-day wear against the jettatura. And besides the neglect of this dervish, have we not shot an ibis, whose outspread accusing form is ever in sight of the river-god imploring mishap upon us?

But to-day, as we hoped, we finally broke the spell. Our sheikh with the stomach-ache, and his hundred men, where usually there is four times that number, at ten leisurely spread themselves on the rocks, waved their batons and flags, and then at last went up the signal cry, the chorus of the men at the ropes. We had but a few feet to go, and we then faced El Bab—the

real Cataract, the last and greatest.   When
I say that it resembled for twenty feet the
least lively part of the rapids at Niagara,
an American can guess that it was something serious for an African river.   And
we had spectators of our triumph.   A
government boat filled with American
officers going on an expedition, with two
cannons and two hundred soldiers into the
heart of Africa, came and admired us.
Their boat flying at our heels, did in two
hours the distance from Assouan, while the
malevolent dervish had detained us seven
days.   And the *Clara* came and looked at us.
We invited two of their number to share the
perils of an ascent, which accomplished, in
return, Miss Dudu shared in the excitement of theirs.   And so by the blessing of
Osiris (the surnamed Lord of the Cataract)
we were free to flutter on to Philæ, and
there breathe our unspoken gratitude near
his grave.   Could we pass Philæ after our
unsatiated hunger, and with such a moon ?
The *Clara* had had a nibble at it on

donkeys, and therefore fled away, but we gladly furled our sails at the foot of a lovely and lofty temple, whose pillars, dark against the sky, hung over us like lotus buds from the river's brink.

We had all the afternoon before us, and the promise of a moon afterwards. The island is the tiniest, loveliest little place ; it cannot contain more than ten acres. And all this space is occupied without crowding, by ancient temples, intentionally divergent from symmetric lines. Palms grow there, and all would be perfect but for the frightful Christian Copt, whose mouldering rubbish insults the departed glory it cannot wholly spoil. On either side the island a temple overhangs the river. The farther one has columns surmounted by unchiselled capitals, which startled us, and we think to see the swarthy artists of old returning before our sight to continue their work— that work the same variations on the grave Egyptian music we had heard the Ptolemy play at Edfoo, and heard here

again—the palm, the fern, and many another
novelty, with exquisite taste, were again
introduced.   We felt the architecture to be
new, as new in a certain sense as a New
York's imitation of Egypt to-day.   Everywhere it is betrayed.   Egypt enforced an
inviolable repetition of her symbols, but
Rome was free—and knew it.   Audacious
knots of the lotus stem—too accurate
marking of the knee-joints — a smile
betraying Europe—the something which
asserts ungenuineness and a simulacrum
—breathe through these lovely halls, which
losing in reality, gained a festive grace
and lightness which was not of the soil.

All was executed in limestone with the
exception of one massive syenite boulder,
which, polished and cut with hieroglyphics,
separated itself from the masonry in which
it was sunk.   The same tiny staircase as
at Edfoo led us to the roof, perfect as
when finished.   Thence the view justified
the glorious claims of Philæ.   To the
west was Biggeh and its ruins, which we

keep for our return ; and behind us, to the east, a long stretch of desert opening between these terrible rocks, which here add real grandeur to their masses—a fringe of palms and vivid selvedges of green cheer our eyes, for a week starved for verdure. There are no old ruins in Europe so perfect as these, and ruin cannot defeat their simple expression. Every block of them tells the same story—everywhere grandeur and simplicity in the forms—every-where, where a face is chiselled, serenity and peace. And this gem of the desert—set like a smile upon the haggard face of nature—gleams lambent with an inner beauty, better even than the nobleness which is its outward expression, for here, like fire at the heart of the carbuncle, glowed that longing and desire of man, that nameless hope of spiritual perfection which, when men dare name it, bore the name of Osiris. Here flowered that divine blossom first, without which man's life would be poor and barren. Gothama for

India, Osiris for Egypt, and Christ for all, were the incarnation—the prophecy of that better life which earth cannot realise.

And so is Philæ indeed sacred. We did not wait vainly for the consecration of the moon. That healer of the day's destruction and defeats looked upon the island, and column and fane again in the smile of Athor lived their perfect life. Pharaoh's Bed, as the lovely temple near us is vilely called, held us long upon its shining terrace. This temple (hypaethal) always unroofed, was roofed for us with that blue and those stars which the men of old imitated so well. They could not bear these ceilings of stone, and tried to escape to the illimitable from night and nature, as did their thought to the illimitable of Godhead from the limitation of earth's life and its symbols.

We found Eugenio from a sketch had been building up a heroic picture of Philæ's golden days. The temple just as we saw it—behind, a train of priests—an adoring populace—dark against the lustrous sky; and below the upright platform, boats, and barges in shadow, a re-creation of an hour of the past—the blessing of Osiris on the rising Nile.

Monday, Dec. 28th, 1874.

The propyla and columns of lovely Philæ looked long and reprovingly at us, as we danced away, between the serrated hills, above, the fringe of palms—below Coptic and Mohammedan churches, at times breathing defiance at each other, above walls pierced for musketry, as ignoble in their architectural forms as their miserable hostility was to the superb serenity we were leaving behind us.

Wednesday, 30th.

We have now been two days in Nubia, and are full of attention to its merits. Its climate, we have been told, is simply perfection, its beauty much greater than that of Egypt, and its men and women graceful in their simplicity of attire, of finer proportions than their brethren below. We shall have something to say on all these points, and meanwhile it is pleasant to record that the "blameless Ethiopians" of the Greeks —for to them this land was Ethiopia—still are blameless in respect of honesty and truth, as compared with the Arabs.

We seem transported to another river. Its blue surface reflected from the heavens above is nowhere the tawny current that we knew before. The river mysteriously diminished—for it has no branches—is no larger than the Connecticut at Northampton. Its banks—no longer superposed layers of finest mud—are one sheet of living green ; sometimes three different plants grow in little belts between the water and the top of the bank, which is usually about twenty feet high. The palms are fewer than they were, and the mimosa, exquisite in delicacy of form and colour, is taking its place. There never were any wild flowers, and the graceful porous water-jug on our table, of antique pattern and breathing coolness, is surrounded only with the flowering bean. And the birds—where are they? Those myriads which danced like motes in the evening's beam? All is silence. Yet at evening one little cry, just as the sun sets, makes itself heard. It is not unlike the whip-poor-will's; it always seems the same bird, for there is but one note, and the bird is invisible. And not birds only, but inhabitants are wanting; and, strangely enough, Egypt's pests—the nameless one and the flea—disappear in this air.

Yesterday we floated through a grand solitude. There was no sign of a living thing. Through the pure air the slightest noise could reach us, yet all was dumb, save where the river's only voice, now a sigh when afar, now a moan when near, the sakia could be heard. It is like a Greek chorus to one of Æschylus's tragedies, with its eternal lament. It is said to be the Ranz des Vaches of the Nubian, and that he pines for it amid the tumult of Cairo. Though the voice of the sakia and the shadoof are the same, it is almost only the sakias we hear now. It is a mournful region. The desert threatens nearer and nearer; cultivation cannot make a successful battle with it as on the plains of Egypt, and looking over the little ribbon of emerald green to the waste beyond, we know the desert must conquer. Therefore, through the sakia's sigh and the far-heard cry of men, we seem only to hear the awful stillness of the desert. And so sad is this life, fading into death, it would not be endurable were it not for the blessed sunshine that gilds not only the wreck of man's magnificence, but can lend its smile to these shores of desolation.

After breakfast yesterday, when our dahabeah fainted in the breathless air against the bank, we climbed the stony hill above, and sat and listened to the silence. All was still, and away from the river, through miles and miles of rocky desolation, not one touch of greenness. Yes; this is a land which is not lovely if loveliness be life, and yet through whose pellucid sky breathes a strange fascination. Here is peace, if anywhere. The last faint rumour of the life we know has died upon the ear. The quiet is a balsam to our feverish spirits, and from the still shores for ever comes that whisper which had such attraction for the old Christians of the Thebaid, saying to them : " Forget the world, and share with us God's rest."

Though the birds are mostly gone, we are not wholly wanting for game. The Nubian hare is a novelty. Under Antonio's hands—whether treated *en civet* or in a pie—it is equally delicious. Last evening I went with Ruskallah to try and shoot some. We walked gingerly through the lines of lupin or on the little raised rims, like piecrust, of the tiny fields of wheat and barley, and finally heard of two hares. As darkness soon came on I returned, but Ruskallah not only stayed so long that we thought he had met with a mishap, and sent Paolo for him, but again went out in the moonlight—but all in vain. And yet this morning we saw a provoking hare dancing along the bank and defying us.

I have good luck with my window-curtain. Whenever at dawn I draw it, I see a ruin, but I must not abuse my luck or the supply will give out. This morning I drew it, and there before my eyes was a lovely pylon, and lines and blocks of beauty. What it was I did not know, and have not yet had time to study up. But there is something charming in this flying salutation to the grandeur that was. It makes us its contemporary, and our familiar nod re-peoples for us old Egypt. And is it not for every one always re-peopled? Does not every one look over the heads of these pigmies of to-day, and seem to see the mighty temples, the long processions, the chant, the festival, and on every face that sweet familiar smile which makes the chiselled faces of the temples alive to-day?

It is a common enough thing to say that the overclose life of the dahabeah is fruitful in quarrels, and that the smallest fissure between associated tempers will widen into such a gulf as love no longer can traverse. We hear of sullenness and alienation bursting in flame, and a quarantine established between friends and relatives; we even hear of travellers sulking in their cabins, or dividing the cabin by a sheet to forbid intercourse. Fortunately, as yet, no such calamity is ours, but we have had intimations of its possibility. Dear little Kiki is put in quarantine below, for naughtiness. Every dahabeah has a pet. Sometimes it is a parrot, sometimes a Japanese spaniel, but more often a monkey. We know of two now on the Nile, and there must be more. Miss Praed, daughter of the illustrious poet who founded the airy school of light poetry—*vers de société*, as the French call

it—so charmingly continued now by Cal-
verly and Locker, has a tiny monkey which
she adores.   It certainly, in its way, is exquisite, with movements which are graceful,
and an appearance of affection ; to be sure
it bites its mistress through her gloves.
But let us try to think the best we can of
monkeys, since Mr. Darwin brought them
to the front as our relations.   At the house
of Mustapha Aga, in Luxor, I saw a little
long-legged monkey—of most Darwinian
profile—and a voice so like that of a suffering child as to seem like ventriloquism.
No mother could have heard it without
resenting this unfair appeal to her feelings.
But our pet is our dear little Kiki.
This kitten has a mysterious faculty of
being everywhere at once.   When shut
in its little prison, it will instantly reappear
at bow or stern, as it may fancy; like a
conjuror it seems to say : " You see me put
that kitten into the hold, and, lo ! you open
a drawer and it is there."   It passes through
panels and doors in a way Miss Katie

might envy, and give doubts to Messrs. Crookes and Varley. Perhaps Bubastis could tell us something of this. I saw at Cairo a pair of cat's eyes which a gentleman took from his pocket. They were from Bubastis, and had belonged to an idol there. The surface was crystal, unirised by time, as glass would have been, and they looked alive ; there was the same look in them that I see in Kiki's eyes when, after some audacious misdemeanour, she gazes at you with the ferocious innocence of her species. And she, too, feels the attractive sun of Nubia—and her springs are like those of a cheetah—and she enjoys her youthful claws at our expense in a way that shows her cousins of the desert are nearer than they were. And, therefore, poor Kiki henceforth must be restrained of her full liberty. But she is brought in as babies are at dinner, and thereby gets an hour of frolic, evidently wondering for what offence this limitation has been made to her freedom, her cathood only using those instincts inevitable to its nature.

Mr. Story, in his striking statue of Delilah, has introduced a razor as her instrument for the cutting of Samson's hair. Many ignorantly have criticised this, but he is wholly right. It is a common idea that Delilah clipped one lock or two, as she might for a love-token, but when in the East every one is clean shaven on the head, with the exception of the tuft of hair by which the angel is to hoist them into heaven, and so like a scalp-lock, which the Indians leave for a quite different reason— is it likely that she would spare any of that in which his strength lay? It is very amusing to watch the process of head-shaving as done in our boat. The razor cuts the hair easily and clean at the root. The razor is dipped in soap-water, but I see no brush or lather. Under a clean turban one's head so shaven must feel delightfully cool. Our hair, perhaps, like the coats of animals, needs its thickness to guard against the cold, and here abundant locks are a nuisance. The imported sheep in the West Indies mostly lose their fleece, but here the sheep have very heavy wool. Its colour is a golden brown or black, and the tent of the Bedawee is dark; thus it may be seen at a great distance when a white tent could not. In this way we may understand the allusion to "the black tents of Kedar."

To-day I saw a sailor rolling something under his heel; I took it, and found it to be hasheesh. It was soft, pasty, and of a greyish-green. This drug, made from the seeds of the hemp, has from time immemorial been the source of those day-dreams the Arabs love so well; it is his substitute for wine, which is forbidden by the Koran; and holy men, feeling its sustaining stimulus, have advocated its use by the faithful. The Arabian Nights' Entertainments is the literature which is the outcome of this dangerous pleasure. We from time to time read a story from the book under this

Nubian sunshine. It takes its place as naturally here as does a palm, nor is there as much hasheesh in the book as we think. Its narrative is as realistic as a tale by Bret Harte or Dickens. The marvels of the child's nursery we find to be the commonplaces of the East. Words are often the history of things, and hold a moral meaning which explains much. The practice of hasheesh smoking is here generally discredited by the better people, and when one knows that our word assassin means hasheesh-eater, one easily sees the cause of this disrepute. If we had a word which connected drunkenness with murder it would have the same terrible significance.

Thursday, December 31st, 1874.

To-day's date is memorable as showing that in our life-voyage we are on the point of entering the new year 1875, and in our Nile voyage we have just passed the line of the tropics. How differently a year counts in Egypt from a year in

America. Can it be that in our two hundred such spaces of time we have built up a nation, overflowed a continent, strung with cities nameless rivers, which in size and beauty may vie with the majestic river we sail upon? Every sand drop in our hour-glass sparkles with vivid life. Cities are destroyed and rebuilt in a year, while in this drowsy air, where centuries look but as moments, time notches the pyramids with but one more indentation, and everything seems always the same. Every month in America sees introduced a new method of shortening toil. Man moulds the matter of the world as if it were wax between his fingers. Here the sublime monotony of the East swallows all human invention. The pictures upon the walls of the oldest temples are in much pictures of Egypt's life of to-day.

This contrast of eternal fertility of thought, with the life destitute of thinking, makes Egypt much beloved of Americans. Here, not only that longing for a visible past, which is denied at home, stimulates imagination and memory, but withdrawal from the terrible activity of business, escape from those grooves of action and habit which tear and wound the spirit, find on these shores a rest which is health to their life.

A day or two ago a sailor, asleep, as they mostly are when not at work, tumbled into the river. The reis bounded, the sailors shouted, but our man, leisurely waking from his dream, swung himself on board again before the current had swept him past the rudder. I don't know whether these Arab sailors swim, but they are always in the water. They jump overboard at the slightest provocation, and with Atlantean shoulders lift our boat when run aground. Below the Cataract shipwreck was as soft as sleep, but here there are rocks, and to feel our light craft crash on one when we are all asleep is a trifle startling, but we are generally off again before we have time to think we are hurt. Last night we bumped for a bit smartly, but soon the reassuring swash sent us off to fresh slumber.

This evening Nubia sustained her reputation. We have about reached that happy place which so flies before the longing invalid; which Murray and the world have fixed upon as having perfection of climate, and it has come and visited us. Living is such a luxury that we think and talk of nothing else. In this dry elastic air, our souls seem to look far and bright, as do the stars which contemplate us. Our moon, always incredibly beautiful, and without that glare of our home moonlight, where the keen light and the sharp shadows try to rival those of day, our moon wanes as it waxed, in the shape of a boat upon an even keel. This dahabeah of the skies, freighted with things lost on earth and worked by mild lunatics, can hardly hold more of dreamland than does our boat below. Nor is it wholly dream, our life. There is a peculiar effort of the mind, which moves like a questing hound among the dim places of the past, and puts up the game of fresh thought and restored life. And either this fatigue of the mind, or the nervous waste of this climate, obliges us to have our dreams well fed.   We are, indeed, slowly eating our way into Ethiopia. Amid the abstinence and sometimes half-starvation on either bank, our shameless dahabeah moves along a line of gourmandise.   And Antonio, resolving the sublimest things, knows that we have invited the *Clara* to dine with us on the New Year.   He is determined to sustain the reputation of Malta above that of Arabia in cooking—but on whom shall he wreak his genius?   The *Clara* has left us—disappeared; and the news brought to us is like that brought to Shylock of Jessica:

> "I often came where I did hear of her,
>   But never found her."

Even yet we fondly hope she will come

to time; if not, woe be upon us! for we, like the Roman girl, will be buried under Antonio's weighty attentions.

New Year's Day, 1875.

At last Nubia has failed us where she is strongest. Perhaps, as children say, " there was not enough to go round;" but the *feu de joie* of the dying year was a failure. Pale, colourless, and dejected the setting sun of December 31st seemed to say—"Goodbye; I'm worn out; let me go."

Every evening at half-past five, like the Arabs, we strike our tent on deck, and it is as the lifting of a drop-scene. But the display is so modest, the magnificence is so chaste and unearthly, that we scarcely dare speak of it with praise. Last evening the river triumphantly reflected back the splendour across the opaline and pearly hues, which held the flower-like beauty of the sky. The river shot its moving threads of blue and silver while focussing

M

the living gold ; upon the bank towered a group of dusky palms, which sent long lines of shadow across the trembling water. And such delight as are these sunsets ; it is too keen to last—soon, only too soon, night folds it in darkness. The stars and we then wait, and not long, for the succeeding pageant, for at last the silver queen mounts the throne the golden king has abdicated. What shall we do without her ? Through these gleaming nights we have had her for a lantern as we sailed, and we shall not dare to grope without her, and thus must linger against the river bank.

The river has again changed its character. Sandstone is exchanged for syenite and the demoniac boulders below Philæ. We seem at times to be floating upon a lake surrounded by mountains. Their colour, purple against the sunset, is of a pleasant yellow when near ; they crowd upon the river, and the few feet of cultivation below them seem man's last struggle with the desert. And when they recede from the river, comes at last victorious, waving its tawny mane like a thirsty lion of the desert, the sand, even to the water's brink. The mountain has come to Mahomet, since Mahomet could not go to the mountain, and the longing wastes of barrenness have brought themselves to the Nile, as the Nile cannot visit them.

As twilight with its mystery wrought fancies on the brain, we thought we saw strange images, like little mummies restored to life, gazing at us from the rocks; and a little farther on we thought we saw a grey fox trotting along the path. Nor were either deceptions. The long-legged grey animal with a bushy tail could not have been a dog, and the weird images were but stones dressed up by children in tatters for lack of dolls. Some children soon came by, so shadowy and strange under those enormous crags, they seemed as unreal as these images; and in the after-

noon I saw what affected my fancy.   I saw
all lonely, upon a spit of sand—no human
being near it—a boy's toy dahabeah, lost
upon this savage shore.   I seemed to be
in Lilliput, and wondered if I had passed
unobserved the tiny cities of such creatures
as could have sailed in her.   And it brought
to mind Boston Common and the Frog-
pond, where little fleets nearer home always
ride in safety.

Near Korosko we had the good luck to
see on a sand-bar three crocodiles.   Two
were together, and I gave one a bullet.
We all thought it hit.   If it did, it was no
more than tapping a snuff-box—but he
and his fellow with a great splash simply
scuttled off under water.   I fired at the
third, and missed, but I had the satisfaction
of seeing him, too, scuttle away, showing it
was no log but a real crocodile.

Soon after this we came in sight of the
Clara, and as she presently had a fair
wind, and we lost her around a point, it
seemed plain that she was running away

from our dinner. None the less did Ruskallah and the cook continue their preparations. Pausing a while against a bank, Eugenio and I did our share of the affair by taking a good walk for appetite. When we came back, the *Rachel* was really beautiful. A profusion of palm branches ran up every iron rod, and sweeping in curves overhead, made of our deck the prettiest dining-room in the world. A water-melon was hung among the leaves, while a gourd, with tracery of crimson sugar, hung over the cabin door ; and besides the thirty pretty coloured lanterns which glowed among the palm branches, Ruskallah had produced superb glass shades for our candles, elaborately cut and ornamented. On this important occasion our second cook — a Nubian, with a smile like honey, and arms that would make the fortune of a prize-fighter— was promoted to be waiter, for this time only. He accomplished this with smiling grace, only expressing occasionally wonder that we did not eat everything. The table was garnished with two imposing structures, one of sponge-cake, the other of nougat, both crested with flags, and both rich with sugar plums and coloured sugar. Antonio had done his best, and each dish was pronounced a masterpiece. A game pie and a turkey stuffed with truffles were particularly noticed. Our best wines were brought out, and our absent friends were not forgotten in our toasts. My dear nieces, for whom this Journal is written, and their illustrious father, were all remembered. As our banquet terminated, we noticed that, below, our dragoman was entertaining a select party, consisting of the handsome reis, the agile Paolo, and our beneficent Antonio. When the eating was over for all of us, we had a discharge of pistols and rockets, the latter perversely running their heads under water, which the Nubians by their glee intimated they considered the correct thing. Soon after the soft hum of the

tarabouka and the drum was heard, and
our sailors, not without their share of
good things, indulged us with antics and
dances, and finally with a grand fantasia,
which rivalled the show of the Nubian
boys a few days since. As our men had
been tracking all day, with difficulty skirting the regimented lupins, and at times
diving under the boughs of the *sant* tree,
which here is of great beauty, streaming
like hair or in gerbs of emerald rockets—
but a moment sufficed to send them from
their fun and activity into deep sleep, and
we, wondering if the *Clara* had dined as
well as ourselves, tried to do the same.
And so ends our great river fête, which we
have thoroughly enjoyed. But we did not
sleep as soundly as our sailors, and at
times could see our belated and vanishing
moon preparing to take its leave. The
Egyptian goddess Athor in the sculptures
carries the moon above her brows and
between her horns. It is thus in Egypt
this goddess wears the moon as the sym-

bol of her universal power, swaying the tided passions as does the moon the tided seas. The Journal takes a New Year's farewell of her in the following lines :—

TO ATHOR.

FAIR Athor, Egypt's queen of love,
Her double queen of love and light,
Stoop from thy shining home above,
And make a Paradise of night.

All love thee, all confess thee queen,
As, girt with many a hand-maid star,
Thy visionary form is seen
Moving in state, serene and far.

Here in this land where all that lives
But symbolises Him alone,
Who the dread boon of being gives,
The unseen, the unimagined one :

Be thou the symbol of the deep
Delighted sense of rest and peace,
Which hangs the poppies round thy sleep,
And dreams with thee o'er land and seas.

Thou healer who canst bid atone
The Day for all the wounds it makes,
And bring from anguished bosoms flown
Again the peace thine own partakes.

Thy smile time's wrecks can touch and gild,
So that each fallen fane is whole,
Ah ! from our ruined lives rebuild
Again the temple of the soul !

Dread Rè, thy kingly spoil are we,
And fly thy splendour as it falls
On fainting hearts, as we may see
Victorious yet on Karnak's walls,

Rameses' falchion flash and smite
Above his flaming chariot wheels,
While pierce those arrows, winged with light,
His breast who suppliantly kneels.

But thou, thine arrows are as balm,
Nor we thy suppliants in vain,
Oh ! shower them from those heights of calm
On willing captives of thy Reign.

Saturday, Jan. 2d, 1875.
DERR.

There are no signs of the *Clara*, though
we hear of her as being here last night.
Derr is the capital of Nubia, though not a
large village ; but it is neat and comely,
being built of mud accurately squared at
the angles, though we did not see even an

unburnt brick.   The Nubian villages are
still more antique in the form of their
houses than are those of Egypt.   The
picturesque upper storey, capped with pottery and fringed with boughs, and pierced
with holes, dove-cotes, in short, for the
pigeons, are wholly wanting.   But in their
simplicity and accuracy of line they often
look like the half-sunk propylon of an antique
temple.   They are neat and clean, for it
is almost impossible to be dirty here when
rain never falls.   Ruskallah went shooting,
and we took a walk under beautiful date
palms, which were set as in pots, so valuable are they.   Often a group springs from
a central trunk in a way we have not seen
before.   The sakias are incessant, rarely
more than fifty yards apart, and make a
pretty picture as the files of dripping
buckets go round, and a child sitting in a
nest of halfeh grass guides the docile oxen
in a circle.   We visited the village and
saw at last something, but not much, of
the Nubian women.   So far from being

naked they were fully clothed in long
dresses of bright blue, and they even wore
trousers.

The fairy creature which seemed to possess the imagination of Coleridge when he
sang of his African maid, who owned a dulci-
mer and sang herself of the Mount Abora,
neither of them had seen, we certainly have
not met. Neither as yet have we found that
ingenuous child of the desert, so maidenly
in her beautiful nudity, and so like a living
statue, which certain clergymen affection-
ately mention. We are on the watch for
her, but she has not yet turned up, but as
the crocodile has, we have patience, and
rely upon Nubia's unfolding all her wonders.
These women of Derr didn't smell very
badly of castor-oil, but they wear their
shining black hair in little twists and braids
which must have come down from the days
of the Ptolemys, for Cleopatra's hair is of
the same fashion. Some of these women
wore black bracelets, rings on their thumbs,
and little ornaments of silver over their

forehead. We saw them turning a circular millstone to grind doura in the most primitive way. In defiance of Murray we were offered nothing for sale, and heard no cry for backsheesh. We met a solitary Greek gentleman, who was glad last night to get a bottle of wine from the *Clara* and a cigar from us. He could talk somewhat in Italian and French, and seemed hungry for chat, and pronounced Derr dull as a place for villagiatura.

Sunday, 3d.

It is perhaps desirable to have such weather as we have to-day to teach us to appreciate the good. All journals dilate to mawkishness upon the sweets of Nile travelling, and few care to remember the bitters. Our tempers to-day have been severely tried, and both among the Howadgi and the sailors what was begun in play got a rough edge before it was over. The cook in a jolly tussle with a sailor tried to throw him over board, and when

I remonstrated, he assured me it was only in play. And not only is the weather capricious when we were assured of serenity, but it is paradoxical as well. A strong wind is blowing due south from the equator, but it is quite cold. Atmosphere is the dress of the landscape, and Nubia, stripped of her gold and purple, is in sackcloth and ashes. All the magic has fled. The cliffs are uninteresting, the palms look like brooms, clouds of sand are flying across the colourless water, and we, in our floating prison, feel the narrowness but more irritating. And yet we remember yesterday's sunset; it seems as far off as if it had visited the Ptolemys. It was simply the most exquisite one we have had. In this pure air the material for clouds is wanting, and were it not for the heavy dews there would be none. During the day, yesterday, silvery lawn, fine as if spun by the fairies, was drawn across the sky, and this, touched by the light of the departed sun, made the whole heavens seem powdered with rose leaves.   No flower, no shell, no pigment, could match its ethereal delicacy.   What evening can make out of to-day's materials for her punctual display we wonder much, but she is too good an economist to try for a surprise which would be so out of keeping with the day and our irritability.   Why this south wind is so cold I cannot find out.   Mountain-snow and glaciers are too far off; there are too many burning wastes between, and it must suffice for us that it is one mystery more in a land so full of them.

If it were not that the north wind usually blows, there could be no Howadgis on the Nile.   Apparently this is caused by an influx from the north to fill the place made vacant by the rarifying air of the Desert.   Without this wind no sail-boat could stem the current; its return, though slow, whatever the wind may be, is at least possible.   It then unships the long-yard, and drifts with what help its little sail may give it with a south wind.   But occasionally there is no wind at all, and then the sweet freshness departs, the sun drops on us as through a burning-glass, and the omnipotent fly pillages and tortures us at his will. For the fly, like the poor, is "always with us," though not in swarms as in Egypt.

Ibreem, Tuesday, 5th.

The sailors think the cause of it is the Nubian pilot we took at Assouan. The truth is we make no progress, but it offers us a fine chance to study Nubia. We have not made more than thirty miles for the last three days, and as the men are fatigued after four hours tracking, we pull up and make explorations. As this south wind continues, and it is cold, these walks are delightful. Sometimes we strike straight into the desert, and soon feel its immensity and silence stretching about us. Here we have real mountains, jagged in outline, and at times solitary and purple against the horizon. One we saw yesterday, with the desert tender with distance,

stretching away from it, was so like a
pyramid that we almost had to consult
Murray to find that we were not mistaken.
No wonder that Nature protects, as having kinship with herself, works of art so
harmonious with her own forms. It is
the excellence imported into a country to
which Nature is hostile. The imagery of
the Bible, the creed which was once a
nation's life, looks scarcely less unreal under
a northern sky than do the forms of art and
architecture imported there. Under this
sun the Bible fuses into a harmonious
whole. Its strange places are easy to
understand. The habits—the atmosphere,
inconceivable by the northern mind, are
those of every day, and like what we see
around us. No wonder to the devout
mis-intelligence of the northern devotee
the Bible should become a fetish ; taken
away from the life which made it fluent it
is hard as iron. And even its super-
naturalism, which we are finding day by
day to be not extra naturalism, but a part

of the machinery of the universe, has to them the same fetish character, and they are shocked to find that a Bible miracle is not a possibility confined only to Judea.

In this purest of airs the eye goes on and on, past hillocks and new levels of sand, till, whether the last faint line of distance be earth or sky, sight refuses to say. To breathe the desert air is a new sensation; it is even better than the air of the river, more elastic and thinner. It was curious to notice the footprints everywhere in the sand. There was that one which astonished Robinson Crusoe, so defined that Leather Stocking by it could have known who left it; the print of the camel, whose form was exactly like that of the marine creature we call the horse-shoe; bird-tracks of all dimensions, and the well-known track of the dog (*kalb*), and much larger ones of quadrupeds, which we delight to believe are night-prowlers—the wild beasts of the Desert.

The sand refused intelligibly to retain

N

the stupendous prodigy of high-heeled boots ; it would only show a scoop for the most beautiful foot in the world. Against the lovely yellow of the sand the rocks under our feet were as purple as a violet, a colour I never saw in stone before.

At other times we skirt the river, in our walks passing under forests of the castor-oil plant, for some grow to the height of twenty feet. The leaves are large indented shields of dark blue-green. Its pretty flower is like a mignonette blossom, and its capsules are the bigness of hickory nuts. How strange is human nature ! the thing we fly from, and from which all our being shrinks, is the favourite scent of the Nubian belles. In spite of all the clergymen's stories, they are intolerably ugly, and they do not need this additional repulsiveness.

The cultivation of these savage people is very perfect. I saw a farmer yesterday admitting his little river, three inches across, into one of the squares of his little checker board. To do this, with his pick he fenced with a tiny wall a saturated square, and then broke down the wall of the one he meant to irrigate. He seemed to be crooning to himself—"Sat prata biberunt," and no doubt Virgil's fields were watered in the same way.

We have seen another crocodile, always on a sandspit close to the water. He slipped in at the sound of the gun. The view this morning from our deck was very striking. Immediately in front of us, on the left, was an enormous buttress of rock overhanging the river, crowned with the remains of a Roman city; below, on perpendicular faces of rock, were tombs. A square like a door marks for a long way these places. Behind us was a beautiful reach of the river, and, faint but clear, in the distance was a green bank and its sakias, all mirrored as in glass—the silver of the river sand, the gold of the desert sand, both keeping their colour as if close to us. And above them floated the prettiest little clouds, ruddy against the blue.

Wednesday, 6th.

A slant of wind last evening enabled us
to sail.   Oh the pleasure of seeing these
anchored shores sweep by! and to hear the
ripple, now more musical than ever.   But
our pleasure did not last long, for the river
here interminably winds, and the next twist
of it brought the wind, as before, over our
bow.   Again to-day, by fits, the same satisfaction of sailing.   A haze which has been
over everything since this south-west wind
blew still continues.   Through it the arid
and wild peaks of Arabia against the sky
are softly stumped in vapour.   This gives
a northern look to the scene.   The high
banks are still one sheet of emerald, and
when, suddenly entering a reach, the trees
come near the bank's edge, we are reminded
of an English park.   Across the river the
wheat fields look like the most delicious
turf, and we long to roll on them.

There has been a good deal said in
books of travel by enthusiasts of the

sound of bells in the Desert. Our favourite writer—that unconscious humorist
—absolutely asserts that he heard bells of
all the churches of New York, and he
carefully notices their different sounds.
A more cautious Englishman also heard
these bells, and after marvelling a little,
discovered the sound came from the wind
ringing in his gun-barrel. We, too, last
evening heard these bells, and musically
beautiful they sounded, clearly ringing
through the twilight — but the mystery
was not far to seek. It was no mystery,
though indeed not without its poetry.
The insatiate wires of the telegraph,
which insist on accompanying us through
these wilds, brought these cheerful sounds
from home. They rang with fitful swells
and pauses, and surely a clergyman, whose
memory is a belfry of such music, may
be excused for hearing with rapture what
he loved so well.

Not to be wanting in *couleur locale*, our
ladies have dyed their nails with henna.

Though it looks very prettily, yet it is somewhat painful to believe, as some have it, that Homer's "rosy-fingered Dawn" is suggested by henna. The sailors put henna upon their hands, as good for the skin, and the better enabling them to row. Seeing the henna paste prepared for them, our ladies thought it good fun for once to try this eastern embellishment, and hoping for the *Clara's* company at the next day's dinner, they desired to produce an impression. And so they went to bed, their finger tips duly swathed in shreds of linen cloth. The next morning the colour had fixed itself for weeks, and we think it very pretty, though by her absence it was lost upon the misguided *Clara*.

This fresh weather reminds us that there is such a thing as electricity in the world. That electricity which acts on human beings is liveliest with us. The secret difference between America and Europe is the greater electrical stimulus of America. There it throbs along every nerve, flashes through every brain, and is as the driving-wheel by which its enormous business engine is moved. It stimulates—it sustains, but it tears. It ploughs great ruts in the habits of life, and makes a freeman its slave. As in a mad-house, the quiet visitor by the mad is deemed the only maniac, so in over-active America the man of leisure is considered the only absurdity. Leisure there is getting to mean loafing. "The rest with dignity" of the Romans but looks to them as bar-room and billiard-room indulgence. The old war-horse of commerce—the fatigued and satiated millionaire—must still, through the hottest and coldest weather, take his turn at the mill, for fear of being left with that most terrible of companions—himself. Like a trout, he must shake his fins in the eddy of business—all else is stagnation and death.

But here there is none of the electricity which drives the brain. Man's life is set in a background of repose; idleness is looked upon as man's natural condition, and thoroughly believed in. This indolence gives grace to the gestures of the Arab. With us all is *saccadé* and angular. Good manners disappear in the rush of action and thought, but out of his Heaven of repose the Arab moves towards you with the grace and good manners of a prince. Hepworth Dixon thinks that freedom and bad manners are identical. In that case, how just is our claim to be free! The wind, which turning favourable, was wafting us on to Wady Halfa, made us certain of overtaking the *Clara* there at night, but it suddenly fell, and we were left helpless and anchored in the middle of the river. Though disappointed, yet as we still faced southward, all Africa seemed open before us, and we know that, Wady Halfa reached, we have seen the end of our voyage and its southern limit. And though our gleaning down the river will be richer than our harvest up it, yet there is something in the flight onward to wild and unknown regions irresistibly attractive to the imagination. We hope to store our wallet with many a new fact, many a priceless treasure, but adventure feels its wings clipped when we but visit what we have already passed.

But before night fell we had seen the supreme glory of Nubia. When the whole right bank was soft in the shadow of the descending sun, flying with all sails set, we came in sight of the stupendous figures of Aboo Simbel. That the men of old should have left so far from civilisation, in desert solitude, such sublime tokens of their prowess and grandeur, captivates the mind. It is the advance guard of art and culture before both fade in the solitude and life-lessness of the desert. At the first cry of " Aboo Simbel!" *lorgnons* were in every hand ; and by the mystery of the lens we were brought face to face with these gigantic forms before we reached them. But soon, with reverent salutation, we flew past the grand cliffs which man has made speak for him for ever. All was soft and shadowy, yet on our mind were stamped for ever the placid and noble figures which have gazed out upon these waters since the dawn of history. Their simplicity, their dignity, their lofty grace, became at once a possession of the mind. There is no complication in the influence of the sculptures of ancient Egypt. What the sculptor meant to express is so plainly told that even our eyes which ran could read. One could hardly refuse to the old creed the solution of life's enigma when expressed with such childlike confidence. Unlike the gods of other faiths, who demand initiation to understand them, these command the adoration of all, nor can it be denied. The appeal to our sensibility is too direct to be escaped, and we gladly believe the highest claims of this old religion which has left for itself such representatives. Of course, though eternal, it was but the impression of a moment— a fleeting glance. Details of expression and workmanship we leave for our return, but we are glad to have this complete though fugitive picture for our memory, for here, as everywhere, first sight goes for so much.

Immediately on passing these majestic lords of the river, the desert sand puts on a new aspect. We had before seen it bursting from its bounds and stifling the difficult culture of the bank. We had seen it pouring in tiny rivulets, each a Pactolus of ruddy gold, in mimic imitation of running water, till it fell into the Nile. But here, between the parted cliffs, the fantastic solitary crags which stood isolated with forms that looked like peaks of fancy, it drove as does a snowstorm in sand-drifts, which, through this tropic glow, brought to mind the snow-drifts of New England. We have all seen such round many a farm-house lane, the same exquisite and waving curve cresting the drift, and the same tortured and fanciful plunges at the end.

The light and shadow on these drifts

were enchanting. The shadow so cool and defined, where the forms were sharp, so tender and melting when rounded, and the sunny yellow between them gained brightness by the contrast. As far as the eye could reach, the lofty cliffs of stone, which till now had held together, were split and divided into hundreds of solitary mountains.

If the region around Assouan looked as we may imagine to look the surface of the moon, this was the country of sprites and goblins. There is nothing like it elsewhere to be seen, and pyramids and castled crags and bastioned fortresses, seemed everywhere reproduced by the freakish hand of nature.

We notice the predominance for many days of the dôm-palm over its more graceful sister the date-palm. The dôm here flourishes and sends out its hundred fans, each looking ready for a lady's use, from the abrupt and spiked boughs; the short stem half-hidden by the wasted and

depending branches which throw fantastic figures in shadow upon the sand. At Elephantine we first tried the dôm-palm's fruit, and were amused to find it, as all have described it, so like ginger-nuts. There is a comic pleasure in these resemblances of things in strange lands with familiar objects at home. The mind feels a peculiar content in classifying any new thing under an old head, so, when I saw a dôm-palm with its seven branches (the largest number I have seen) curving outward, I was reminded of the seven-branched candlestick on the Arch of Titus, and instantly the palm became familiar by the comparison.

Many travellers have spoken of the sand here as reminding them of the snow, but the last traveller must not be denied the expression of his pleased surprise. And we are in the country of the sakias. Its buckets go up and down before our eyes for ever. Through the night and through the day we hear its cry, and when we say that it sounds like the moan of a thousand camels, we feel comforted and at home with it, though so lately the camel was a stranger to us.   We have just seen four grey camels standing motionless upon the bank, while, below, their owner gathered for them grass at the water's edge.   They were so thin and worn these poor camels!   Their hind legs, which always look as though held to the body by a peg, seemed ready to come off, and when one of them turned and faced us, he looked cut out of paper, so thin and shadowy he was.   Mr. George William Curtis thinks the camel looks conceited, but I can hardly fancy such a feeling in the heart of this poor companion of man in his most solitary and desolate conditions.

Part Second.

Friday, 8th.

WE arrived at Wady Halfa in good time, and were pleased to find the familiar *Clara* again associated with us. She had arrived soon after ten the same day. We interchanged visits and got all the last news of our friends. Though they had a run of sixty miles after leaving us at Philæ, they had, as we, the wind in their face, and tacked slowly. It seems that though we saw the *Clara* with her lifted sails the day of our dinner, we were invisible to them, perhaps because ours were furled.

We could see little or nothing of the village of Wady Halfa, yet there were signs of business and activity about us. The expedition under the American officers had ordered seven hundred and fifty camels, and they were in a great camp across the river, dotting the plain, and looking very African indeed.

As Wady Halfa is the southern terminus of our journey, or rather the rocks of Abouseir upon the Second Cataract, it was important that our last impression should be a lasting one. It was all that we could desire. The day for our trip there was perfect, a breeze tempering the freshness, and the sky blanched at the horizon and alive with light. We combined with our friends of the *Clara,* and soon after breakfast rowed just across the river, where the camels and donkeys were awaiting us. Our little caravan consisted of six camels and eight donkeys, each party carrying its own lunch.

This first intercourse with a camel had long been looked forward to and was very interesting. The camel is a creature unique in its merits and defects, and I should suppose Mr. Darwin would consider it a favourite proof of natural selection and the struggle for life. It alone of man's conveyances has elastic pads to its feet, and all appliances for desert travelling. Its eye, protected in its bony socket, tells of the melancholy solitude it lives in, and its mouth, with its projecting upper lip and drawn in at the corners, gives it a look of great wisdom. It reminded me of one of our western senators locking within himself that knowledge which his constituents must take on trust. It seemed to be able to tell many a secret if it chose. Our plucky ladies were soon hoisted into the air, the camel rising through three-jointed movements, which shook them up considerably. But they looked very imposing when perched aloft upon their wooden saddles, the colour of the lovely rugs relieving the grey of their dresses. So away we went on our little ride through the desert, feeling as important as if we were pilgrims to Mecca. I had as usual a capital donkey, and I stuck to it. All donkeys in Egypt bear to the

O

left, but if let alone will finally bring themselves into file. There was one tiny donkey from which the legs of a gigantic Nubian depended till they grazed the sand, and behind him, why I could not imagine, was his little boy. And yet that donkey never flinched, and at the end came in with the rest. There were the porters, buried behind their lunch-baskets, and of course a tail of natives. The ride was a very pleasant one, and we had no mishaps. Once a camel stumbled with Miss Greene, our leader of the hounds, but she was not to be so caught, and, soon accustomed to their seat, she and Miss Dudu would strike into a spirited trot, to the envy and admiration of all.

We arrived at Abooseir unfatigued, and while lunch was getting ready we mounted the crest of the cliff and gazed. If Nubia wished to stamp herself into our memory she had succeeded. The view was the most striking thing we have witnessed on our journey. Washing the foot of our precipice, tortured between countless rocky islands, with many a swirl and billow below us, swept the Nile. On either side are sandstone rocks, but all the rocks of the river-bed are black as coal. We were not sure, but thought them basaltic; for here and there were marks of columnar structure. It was plain no boat could ascend, as the water now is, these seven miles of cataract, but future travellers will probably find a way to have their dahabeahs carried above them by railroad. Upon these ebon islands here and there grew a stunted mimosa—a heron immovable on a sand bar we watched during our stay, but it never stirred. What the good Paulo had prepared was not lost on us; our appetite was whetted with our two hours' ride, and sitting in the shadow of the rock, we looked over our cold turkey a thousand adieux to this stupendous land of beauty married to horror. At our leisure, afterwards, we examined the rocky album, where so many names are inscribed, and we saw many a name made dear to us in Egypt; foremost, Belzoni's, and poor Elliot Warburton's, illustrious among others unknown to fame. There was Lord Dufferin's, and the Empress Eugénie's, and Cook's—could he be that great man who throws over the earth his travellers by handfuls? His menagerie is rarely brought as far as this; we dodged it at Assouan *en route* for Philæ, thinking too many cooks spoilt the broth.

Mr. Porcher had the good luck to find already cut the name Porchera. By obliterating the "a" he entered into possession. Miss Dudu bravely cut her name in full, and we were willing to let so fair a representative suffice for the *Rachel.*

We trotted back in the cool of the afternoon, and some camels were exchanged for donkeys, as being too great a luxury to be monopolised. Something was said about "purgatory" by somebody, but it is probable no reference was meant to the noble camel. We passed enormous squares of merchandise, and solid looking merchants sitting near them. We were offered a small crocodile for sale, sundry light fans, a dagger, but not the splendour we had expected. We had passed the usual bones of camels, which we have always seen in every picture of the desert, but not the five gazelles of our gallant and reverend favourite.

The ladies were soon off their camels. Miss Greene remounted hers to be sketched by Eugenio. The camel shuts himself up like a jack-knife, and looks ready trussed for the spit when one dismounts. On his body, what is not camel is callous; there is one at the top of each of his forelegs on the inside, a large one on his stomach between, and two on the inside of the thighs of the hind legs. These are where he presses the sand in his usual posture when recumbent.

On reaching the *Rachel* a vision of beauty looked at us from the upper deck —a female face whose beauty was not that of Egypt.   She was a Syrian bride, with such exquisite teeth, so delicious a nose, and such a pretty toss to her head, which the orange buds still graced, as even her European dress of frightful purple could not destroy.

Saturday, 9th.

Last night, waking up at half-past three, I put my head out of my cabin window and saw the glorious Southern Cross shining just above the horizon. The Cross is a Latin one, consisting of four stars; three of them may be considered to represent the nails of the Crucifixion.   All was still, and the heavenly host was mirrored in the glassy surface of the river.   The faint and wavering image of the Christian symbol was earth's reflection of the sublime and everlasting truth secure in Heaven.

The beautiful Syrian we admired so has for a husband a merchant who is taking her to the Soudan.   We bought of him some anisette to remember her beauty by, and would have kept a box of vermuth, but it was not satisfactory. Near us lay a small native boat, in which were strange sheep from the Soudan. It looked as if the pattern for the animal had been lost there, and nature filled up the sketch from bits which she could find. The head was small like that of a gazelle, the legs long and bony, and the tail, which reached the ground, was like a cow's. The dahabeah with the American officers arrived last night, and we only got a peep at these gentlemen as they strolled upon the sand. They go into camp here for three weeks, and all the multitude of camels we see is theirs. We should have much liked to have talked over the plans and projects of their picturesque journey, but fate and our dragoman at nine o'clock said "good-bye" to Wady Halfa, and, sorrowing, we turned our faces northward.

When the wind rose and blew in our faces, we still more wished we had stayed to chat with our countrymen. No good

omens waited upon our departure, and
to-day, Tuesday, the 12th, sees us but little
advanced on our way. The Nile has been
showing us its pleasant side, but now it is
rough as an enemy. Whichever way the
wind blows, it contrives to blow from a
cold quarter. It has ranged below fifty,
and rattles through all our crannies. The
rudder screams in distress, and we are
forced for shelter under the bank, for when
we put off we whirl about helpless in the
current, and lose rather than gain. The
sailors at evening warm themselves at a
fire on the bank, and make a picture like
one of Gerardo della Notte. They row a
little every day to warm them up, and to
keep their hand in, but with no great result. We barely keep up our spirits ; but
Ruskallah breaks in a storm of Arabian
wrath over the Nubian pilot's head, who
rather likes these delays, and when, with a
wink, he said that our dragoman secretly
did too, Ruskallah thundered and lightened.
So we splash on a bit, and the pilot bumps

us on a rock, and the imitative *Clara* doing
the same, thinks she has sprung a leak.
But our delay has been cheered by a
pageant. The day before yesterday there
seemed to be a regatta on the Nile—an
American regatta. Five noble dahabeahs,
fortunate with the wind which baffled us,
drove by splendidly, the American flag
flying over every stern. The race was
led by our unfortunate friend from New-
buryport, whose dragoman has died on
this passage. After this the little fleet of
General Maclellan, all close together, followed. Discharges of guns, wavings of
handkerchiefs, and cries of welcome, were
interchanged as they successively shot by.
Never have we seen dahabeahs sail like
these, and it made a lovely picture. And
to think of the news we missed, which
they carried by, and which we may long
wait for. We have had no letters, no
newspapers, for a month, and this truce
with the outer world gives us a deeper
sense of the remoteness of Nubia.

But if we cannot sail we can walk. Sometimes we promenade the bank, marching on its gigantic steps till arrested by a sakia trough or the prickly barrier of a mimosa; sometimes we strike into the desert, tasting the silence as we go. On the high rocky crests we are amused picking up agates and pebbles, which the desert rounds, as does the sea, and bits of petrified wood, which we bring away with us. Sometimes we straggle into a Nubian village, and watch the oily women grinding their doura, and we buy of them their silver bracelets and their massive ear-rings. We see everywhere cresting the sand hills a tree like the larch, faint blue in colour, and we bring home branches to adorn our mirrors. Sometimes we come, near the water, upon mysterious mounds of unexplained origin. They consist of a kind of turf overgrown with grass, and are seamed with what looks like rock, but which our canes pierce easily. Are they of yesterday, or did the little temple which our

friends of the *Clara* stumbled on to-day,
and which bore the cartouche of the great
Rameses, know them as coeval? As Murray knew not of the temple, so he and even
the learned Mr. Heath fail us. But we
love this uncertainty. Time, like space,
should have its blue distance; the indeterminateness of the past is the poetry of the
present.

Thank God! the cold kills our last insect enemy. At one time, after sunset,
clouds of midges would in an instant cover
the dinner-table, and flap in every plate.
I have even seen a table in a minute
covered half-a-foot high with them. We
are glad to remember that Shakspeare
says

"Travellers ne'er did lie,
Though fools at home condemn them."

In the way of the plagues of Egypt, I
have seen a solitary toad and a solitary
locust. The locust looked like an impressive grasshopper with a twisted end to his
long body, and his big wings seemed made

for those desert flights which are sometimes the terror of this land. The only
snakes we have seen were the harmless
cobras of the snake-boys at Cairo.

Tuesday, 12th (*continued*).

In the afternoon we visited the little
temple we had heard of. It was quite
treasure-trove, and seemed wholly our own,
as no one speaks of it. Though very
small, the wall being not more than twelve
feet high, surmounted by the dry bricks
we see everywhere defacing the grandeur
of the past, yet the figure of Rameses had
that indescribable greatness which does
not demand space. The two clusters, each
side of the doorway, of Nubian captives
had profiles very characteristic of the race.
I had bought that very morning a silver
ear-ring identical in pattern with those in
their ears. We made out the cartouche of
Rameses the Second very well, thanks to
Murray.

Wednesday, 13th.

This day was made memorable to us by our return to Aboo Simbel. We arrived there in good time to see the sublime façade, softened in the afternoon light, look its best. We were not long in toiling through golden sand which reached nearly from the temple to our boat. Before we entered the temple, on a level with the faces of the statues, we gazed, as have so many thousands, upon the placid beauty of these Titans. We were breathless with toiling in the sand, and gladly fell into it, enveloped in the same shadow which took from the temple the sharpness of its lines. It was delicious to lie in repose and look upon those countenances whose calm the vexations of earth never reach—finished as miniatures in the soft smoothness of their cheeks, and with the true proportions kept where the artist ventured beyond all experience. We felt here that Egypt was at its best. The craving for indestructibility, which the dry, serene sky so befriends, has here found its complete satisfaction. Man has allied, identified himself with Nature's own indestructibility; he has stamped himself into the everlasting hills, and shares their life.

We had time to visit the temple in full light, feel the reverence which we could not escape before the majestic Osirides, and advance with ever-increasing awe till, at the end of the third chamber, the adytum, four featureless, mysterious figures, a faint tremble of colour yet upon their limbs, looked at us from the twilight rather as spiritual presences than any thing made by man. All that we have seen to hush in reverence the soul in temple or cathedral was as nothing before the terrible vagueness of these forms. We seemed, indeed, passing from the judgment-seat of Osiris into the realm of spirits. The terrible indeterminateness of those faces, from which we could neither win a frown or smile, was more impressive than could have been any countenance which art could furnish. Penetrated with adoration and terror, like Dante we found the blessed sunshine was yet that of our own earth, and were grateful to breathe once more the delicious evening air. Before we went to bed plans were formed for an early visit to the temple. The morning light with its horizontal beam lit it all, but could not add to the sublime effect of evening. Yet there is so much to be seen on the walls where Rameses in so many ways placates the deity, the beautiful outline with unerring accuracy expressing the whole thought of the artist, that we are glad to have this help to our study. And there are colours faint and obliterated, yet lingering everywhere. The ceiling is filled with black, and bracelets and ornaments of black, which we have not before seen, adorn the figures.

Thursday, 14th.

There has been a trouvaille by Mariette Bey very near the temple. Behind walls of unburnt brick which there, in their insignificance, look like a hornet's nest, a small tomb about twenty-five feet by fifteen was discovered last year. On the inside, over the door, is written " Opened February 16th, 1874, by A. M." Apparently some graceless wight has obliterated the word Mariette. It is a poor return for M. Mariette's devotion and toil ; his name by every traveller should be exalted as his best friend, and not defaced.

It is now well known that the temples were but the expression of a conqueror's exultation through ceremonials which were only shared in by those of the royal family, the priesthood, and perhaps his leading officers. By them the sacred inner meaning of their rites was monopolised—the people did not share it. It is in the tombs that we are to look, as with the Etruscans, for those details of daily life which for us revive the past. Not only this conservative climate, but the habit of accurate drawing make these tomb-pictures clearer than could be words to bring us near them.

This recently opened temple is so filled with carefully painted objects—the colour still fresh—that in it we have felt ourselves nearer than ever to these ancient men. One picture, in which the nicest details of drapery are mostly retained, represents Rè seated holding the Taw, and wearing four blue bracelets. Under his seat, which has a modern look, there are painted seven more of these emblems. To him a king gracefully offers wine, holding a blue phial in each hand. His head-dress, striped with gold and white, is clubbed behind and falls in a lappet on each shoulder. This lappet and those stripes, of a material plainly as light as silk, we know in Egyptian sculpture as the bands which rise from the forehead of the king, and the lappet expands, as in the great Sphynx, to the banded gigantic masses on either side, which add so much grandeur to the face. The modern kufia is the continuation of this head-dress. This king wears a necklace of seven rings. Before him, on a stand

P

very like a tea-pot without a handle, is the bowl for libation. Behind this, and unsupported, rise stems with the buds and flower of the lotus. The colours of this flower, white shaded with blue, the green of the leaves, yellow where the flower joins the stalk, convinced us that the famous lotus must have been very like our water-lily, and in America I have seen in summer a party of ladies holding them to enjoy their scent, as we see painted upon the walls of Thebes. All details here are interesting, but it is impossible to give them. Let of these two figures only suffice to show how much space it would take to notice all that we admire. On each side was the funeral boat, with that strange slanting line which traverses its cenotaph. In one picture this line is painted across, and has a fringed pattern. Round the prow of the boat were wreaths of peculiar form. We saw a little face, unlike any other we have seen, looking in front, and retaining the freshest colour. Wasps, ducks, and a hundred more objects looked so freshly painted that they might have been done yesterday. There was a vulture with both wings depressed that we have not seen before, holding in its claw an amulet upon which was the Taw. The gaiety, the cheerful colour, the fulness of detail in this tomb separates it from the bare horror of our modern Christian ones. It speaks of good cheer and the life continued without the terrors which surround death for the modern Christian.

Just opposite our dahabeah was a temple to Athor. Those strange masks of faces, so unlike the human face, strike one at once on entering. Why they were made so wide and so shapeless I cannot divine, but beyond them, in other sculptures, is to be found the soft sweet face of Athor such as we have known it. She looks a most unsensual Goddess of Love, as though passion were cooled "in the chaste beams of the watery moon,"—that moon which lies between its clasping horns. " like the

old moon lying in the new moon's arms."
Who can doubt, seeing as we do now
this nightly spectacle, the poetry of old
fashioned a goddess fit to wear the moon
like a pearl on her forehead—"too fair for
worship, too divine for love."

And yet, upon the stomach of a stately
colossal Athor, we find written the name of
one of those Frenchmen whom the world
remembers—no less a name than Lesseps.

At night our men lit a fire in the temple
and sang. The light would flash out into
the night and brighten the smiles upon the
six figures' faces, which would have been
colossi but that those of the temple to Rè
dwarfed them. The men slept in the
temple, and should have had dreams such
as had Joseph in the day when men
believed in dreams.

To escape the ruck of dahabeahs we got off
early, waving our farewells to the everlasting
ones. When we are dust, when the United
States may have broken like a bubble, these
will still smile as serenely as now.

THE COLOSSI.

Benignant, calm, majestically grave,
Earth's childhood smiling in their lifted eyes,
While the hoar wisdom which the dead years gave
Upon each placid brow engraven lies—
Two on the plain and Four beside the wave
Keep watch and ward above the centuries.

　　As is the sand which flies, our little lives
Glitter and whirl a moment and are gone ;
A day it lives, then to Oblivion drives
The haughtiest empire and the loftiest throne :
Swiftly to all the appointed hour arrives,
Men—nations pass, but they remain alone,
Mute in the azure silence of these skies,
Immortal childhood looking from their eyes.

Sunday, 17th.

There may be seen hanging about our
pantry a young man of grave expression
and Nubian countenance, who is a stranger
among us. Nature has not favoured him
as to beauty, but he looks good and trust-
worthy. He is a Christian, and wears
European clothes. His duty is supple-
mentary to the services of Paolo. Though
new to us, he can already hand a plate, and

he has hopes of blacking boots.   He re-
joices in the name of Aboo Simbel.   His
story is this : the order had been given,
Friday morning, to escape the ruck of dahabeahs of General Maclellan's party, to
start early ; but we did not move, for, instead, a great clamour and outcry arose on
the bank, and our Nubian pilot, in sympathy with it, refused to leave.   The fact
is, a young slave escaping from his master
had sought shelter with us, and Ruskallah
Assoun, a British subject, with an English
wife, would not deny protection to a slave.
So the master thundered from the bank,
our pilot scowled from the forecastle, and
time was wasted.   At last Ruskallah, rising with the occasion, in defiance of three
efforts to run away by the pilot, said that
nothing should bend him ; that with one
hand upon the flag of England and his
revolver in the other, he would even blow
the Khedive out of the water if he dared
to demand his protegé.   To give a finish
to the scene, I came flying in my night-

ABOO SIMBEL.

clothes to the pilot, and blazing with Arabian vengeance, and shaking my fist in his face, ordered him under pain of death to start, which he did at once. His wrath smouldered in the breast of our villanous pilot, and rescues were feared along the shore through his connivance.

On the evening of the second day after our departure, at Korusko, the pilot brought down the governor's son, with a crowd at his heels, to reclaim our boy; but Ruskallah said he would shoot the first man who dared to cross our plank; and when the governor's son suggested that we should delay for the decision of his father, Ruskallah proudly replied — "If your father has anything to say let him come after *me*, for we know that we have the law on our side." Nor is this the first time a slave has sought our protection. On going up the river another boy of about the same age wished to stay with us; but then it was thought best to refuse him. Oddly enough, I had thought as a name for our new protegé of Aboo Simbel, where he found us; but Ruskallah had already decided to call him by that name. Our lad has ventured to decide upon being a Christian; and when, yesterday, we brought him out to the excited crowd, and he said " I am a Christian" they laughed, and cried " then we don't want you !" For your Nubian is not wanting in humour.

This is the height of the Egyptian season, and we thread through a line of dahabeahs a few miles apart. The most interesting one was that poor dahabeah at Korusko, wedged between two rocks, and fairly wrecked within twenty feet of the shore. Though she was lightened of everything she could not be moved. Fortunately her party consists of six gentlemen, and no lady. They have sent for the boat of the American officers gone above. We fired a gun over the carcase as we passed, and a shot answered us from the bank, while an American dahabeah waved a handkerchief from a cabin-window.

When dahabeahs meet thus there is often much racing about of sandals and little boats, as this whole fraternity of dragomen, waiters, and cooks is but one great Corporation of the Nile. They have common interests and common acquaintance. Our cook has just seen his brother-in-law go by in sleeves of Tyrian purple, and Paolo seems to have friends in every boat.

This travelling is no small affair, and in a good season there must be between two and three hundred thousand dollars worth of property afloat in the service of the howadgis.

Our party visited a very pretty temple at Amada, with figures of Osistasen, so ancient that it even modernises Aboo Simbel! What a mere fetish of man's fancy is this time after all! All lives are contemporaneous, perhaps, in the eyes of those whose habitation is eternity. Here it is always the same human being with the earth under his feet and Heaven above him, for the mere date of his birth counts for little.

At Ibreem in endeavouring to scale the rocks which separated us from the tombs there, I managed to wrench a muscle, so that, cut off from excursions, I lie on the sofa taking arnica and water, and envying my agile companions. And this is bad luck where temples start up on us sometimes two or three in a day; and though we must, it is distressing to miss any.

Tuesday, 19th.

We resisted the invitation of Wady Sabroah to visit its Androsphinxes and its temple by Rameses, as well as the hypæthral temple at Maharraker, but Dakkeh we could not resist. We were doubly pleased with the souvenirs there of Candace, one of the queens of our fancy, and King Ergamun, who so bravely overthrew the priestcraft that weighed on him, nor for that neglected the gods. The temple is picturesque, and its propylons stately. There is much difference in the sculptures of different rooms of the temple. While, upon the front, Athor retains the severe grace of the good period, the figures farther on are almost ignoble, different in height and with legs like porters. The ladies climbed to the top of a propylon, and found the view superb, while I enviously limped about trying to comfort myself with a sketch. In the afternoon we reached Gerf Hasseyn. I scrambled up to its lofty rock-built temple, and again adored the grand lines of the time of Rameses. We there found colossal figures lining the first chamber, and in the adytum four seated figures, which vividly reminded us of Aboo Simbel. There was the same grandeur, almost oppressive, and the surface of the walls, crusted with white, has well retained the outlines of the bas-relief.

In the village below, Ruskallah produced for us the grey father of his Nubian servant at Alexandria. He is one of twenty-four children, which does not look as if Nubia were depopulated.

At night we tasted, almost for the last

time, the deep sweet Nubian sleep which
gives us a rest with something of the
serenity of its skies ; and even its dreams,
those posters over sea and land, do not
weary us with the journey.   We have
heard of the mud-baths and the sand-baths
of Egypt for sufferers instead of bromide—
let the sleepless try the sleep-baths of
Nubia.

At night we found the *Clara* and Mr.
Tod's boat ; the latter, like a beneficent
fairy, furnished us with five dozen of claret
and the learned book of Mr. Sharpe on
Egypt.

One of Nubia's most glorious days made
our visit to the double temples at Kalabsheh
more than a double pleasure.   There is
all the difference between them of youth
and age.   The smaller temple, built by
Rameses Second, famous for its columns
(the fathers of the Grecian-Doric) and the
victories of Rameses, has that virginity of
the mind, that nobleness inspired by faith,
which the other wholly wants.   Vainly did

Augustus pillage from a predecessor those beautiful blocks and pile them in skilful order. A fate like that which defeated the rebuilding of the temple of Jerusalem seems to have precipitated them down at once in chaotic ruin. With difficulty could we clamber over the prodigious masses. Nothing explains this overthrow but the vengeance of the gods, while above it still sits secure the rock-hewn temple of the true faith, which neither nature nor man could spare.*

Rameses suckled by a goddess is so touching and tender in its action that we are not surprised to find that the sculptor of one of his victories could, in a few lines, so fill us with pathos, as we looked upon that poor mother preparing the supper for her slaughtered son who shall never return, and whose little brother comes flying under the fruit-trees to tell her the sad

---

* The temple was ruined by the Mahometans, who burnt out the Christians sheltered there, the fire thus splitting the stone.

news.   There is something in genuineness which has but one face.   The cleverest make-believe can never take in the spectator if the artist himself disbelieved in his work.   These Romans are everywhere simulating Egypt, but Egypt knows them not.   Their hollow, dead imitation of a religion once alive painfully reminds us of ceremonials in our own day from which all flavour of genuineness has passed away. They are both but the echo of an echo.

A thorough bit of picturesqueness is the little ruin of Gertasse, which we passed in the afternoon without visiting.   It lifts itself with that pathetic beauty which belongs only to death, with its few columns and the mighty slab across them, shafts of gold in the evening light, and with that impressive solitude around it which makes even a ruin in a city so commonplace.

Our sailors had rowed bravely through the lovely weather.   Nearly all day, like a coin of silver, the moon was waning above us and keeping all her splendours for Philæ, which so deserves them. Soon the columns, so highly exquisite, of Pharaoh's bed rose from among the palms, and the two great propyla, each like an ingot of gold, beckoned us forward. But we were not to sleep at Philæ but at Mahatta, to secure the right of first descending the Cataract, for the Chief of the Cataract lives there. Ours was the first traveller's dahabeah to ascend it this year; for this winter at least we can say with Coleridge's Mariner—

"We were the first that ever burst
Into that silent "—river.

And again we are the first to descend. Moonlight belongs to Philæ as it does to Karnak. It needs no romance to feel the wizard poetry of the spot. The rocks which shut it in are incredibly fantastic. Men and animals turned to stone, ghostly hints of the gigantic figures which old Art apparently copied from them; here Osiris grasping his crook and flagellum; there the Sphinx and Memnon, all doubly suggestive in the moonlight, looked down upon the rushing waters. Below, Biggeh and its broken arch, with here and there an upright shaft, was on our left; while on the right rose from the waves the walls of temples which glittered above our heads.

Mahatta, 20th.

The goodwill of the Chief is secured, and he has smoked the pipe of peace with our dragoman. In our sandal we rowed through the plunging water, and began with Biggeh, which we had not seen. What a picture for Gérome was its little temple; a hut plastered into it, where crouched Arabs over their household fire, their strange utensils and themselves relieved against the clean cut stones, the delicately chiselled capitals, and the graceful arch which towered over them. Even for us it made a sketch which we shall prize for ever. Then rowing across, we lost ourselves in the intricacies of Philæ. All the beauty was there, but the strangeness had gone. We are now as much at home in an Egyptian temple as we should be in an American church. They are all alike and perfectly intelligible. We pass between the propyla, through the court with columns, sometimes two, to the inner chamber, to the shadowy silence of the adytum, whose altar, even if its seated figures are destroyed, yet remains.

When, twenty years ago, at Athens, Pittaki made me place my eye at the extremity of the platform on which stands the Parthenon, and what I thought flat I saw to be an arch, and afterwards the columns which seemed perpendicular I found all to incline inwards, keeping that truth to the eye which the formality of right angles cannot,—for the first time I learned that, in architecture at least, mathematical exactness and beauty are not the same.

And I remembered the façade of the Doge's palace pierced by windows intentionally irregular, and the Madeleine at

Q

Paris, a modern Parthenon robbed of its rocky platform and its curves, so, failing in impressiveness; and therefore I am not surprised that Egypt had also its own idea of symmetries made piquant by variety. As the men of old had departed from the upright line in their propylon, so they avoided the formality of parallel lines in walls of the same temple. But Philæ, cramped in its boundaries, is the completest expression of this love of irregularity. There was inevitably so much restraint in the appointed form of their temples that not being able to escape, as the Gothic does, into fantasy, they relieved the severity by these divergencies from the formal.

We retired weary but not satiated from our enjoyment of the place, which in every way seems to us, perhaps, unique among the famous places of the world.

In the evening I took a stroll among the merchants of Mahatta. What beautiful men they were! with their firmly chiselled

lips, most un-African noses, and dark,
childish eyes. What a foreground it was
for a marine painter ! There were elephants'
tusks wrapped in buffalo skins, huge
bundles of dates, mats and carpets inter-
strewed among camels, who went and
came, and, strangely enough, many boxes
of absinthe, which looks as if Khartoum,
like Cairo, in its vices emulated Paris.
We went to buy a lovely antelope, with
lofty straight horns, and eyes seemingly
washed with asphaltum. After the usual
bargaining the price was agreed to, but
when we took the creature the bargain was
repudiated. There is nothing on earth so
uncertain as the value of anything here,
and agreement seems not to clinch a bargain.

21st.

We arose bright and early to breakfast
before the cataract of men fell on us, which
precedes the cataract of water. But as
these new men stretched to the oars, and
we shot away, we turned eyes of passion-

ate regret on that Philæ which was fading from them, and which they may never see again.

PHILÆ.

O Nubian moon, the silence is it thine
Which follows us by this enchanted shore ;
Haunting thy shadows' gloom as they incline
Like basalt shafts prone on the ivory floor ?
    A peopled silence, where old shapes divine
In long procession pass each sculptured door.
Nor wholly voiceless, for each rustling wave,
Trembling mimosa, and dim palmy crest,
And the low zephyr lingering by his grave,
Who needed not its dark oblivious rest,
Whisper——till every silent architrave,
And stately pilon own the immortal Guest,
And the wave bears it as its waters pour,
Murmuring Osiris through the Cataract's roar !

Our vessel slid along as one plunging to its doom. The space before the final descent was enough for us to collect our nerves and prepare for the dangerous enjoyment before us. Our fate depended upon one unknown hand on the tiller, but that one had the experience of years. We crouched where we could to give range to the helmsman's eye, and only the absorbed Antonio escaped the nervous eagerness of the moment.

On, on we drove, and at last, between ridged billows of headlong water, between rocks on either side, which even the oars touched, we gloriously came. The whole passage, from the start to the oily safety below the fall, must have been no more than half-an-hour. As the Nile now is not low, our descent, though glorious, had not the terrors we read of in books of travel. But one ridge of the wave fell in on us, drenching Miss Dudu's cabin and Ruskallah's stores. We shook hands all round in congratulation, and patted the sheikh on the shoulder. Our sailors on the upper deck brought their instruments, and sang the song of rejoicing till driven thence by the sheikh, who wanted the room. Soon were we lying like a hero after battle by the bank at Assouan, which we remember of old. The *Clara* came bravely down, though monkey Mab danced about, and bit everybody in its fright, and the rest got half a scare as the dahabeah whirled about headlong up stream just below the fall.

Saturday, 23d.

Longing for Ombos we made our reluctant reis leave Assouan the evening of the 21st. His reluctance was justified by the poor *Clara*, which stuck three hours between two rocks, which, with the wind blowing, our reis had feared to pass. Morning gave us the beautiful approach to Kom Ombos, which we saw at the same hour from the other side before. We have spent two days here, as it is a favourite spot of artists, and the irrepressible Eugenio, not content with his half-dozen sketches, yet wished a more thorough one. The temple not only stands majestically above the river, but is so richly concentrated into its noble architraves and columns, half-buried in the sand, that its claims are irresistible to a sketcher. There is something pleasant,

too, in its double dedication to Light and
Darkness, Savak, the ghastly crocodile,
being chosen as the emblem of the latter.
He has another temple, as is proper, nearer
the river, all to himself, which we with
difficulty made out. Only one pylon
remains, but suffices as a grand landmark
far and wide. We found the ascent
blocked, and thus we lost the fine view
from its top. It seemed to have no holes
for the masts which bore the banderol, and
which are so noticeable at Edfoo. This
mast and banderol, like so many other
things, Egypt gave to Europe, but
America has not learned to borrow it.
On our fête-days and fairs, the lofty pole
and long streamer would be a real addition
to the flags we hang everywhere.

We have repeatedly lounged about the
temple, and have rejoiced to find on the
ceiling the celebrated canon of measure
for the figure. Apparently the artist had
made a mistake, drawing in red his figures
diagonally, not lengthwise, as the finished

figures are at right angles with these lines.
Two slabs are so connected. In one
Athor, like Diana, holds a bow in her
hand, probably a late conceit. On the
other a spirited figure, with the crown of
Upper Egypt, looks at her over his
shoulder. The drawings are divided into
squares, inconveniently many to count,
such as artists now use when copying a
picture. We were delighted to find also
a sorcerer, holding in each hand a snake
like a walking stick. It brought the old
snake story to mind, and it seems that
even yet snake-charmers by pressing the
head of the snake can induce coma, and as
everybody carries a rod in Egypt, sorcerers
included, they pass off the stiffened snake
for their rod. A German professor has
shown that the trick of the chicken holding
his beak to a chalk line is done by coma,
induced by the awkward position of the
head.

Our boat is rapidly becoming a floating
menagerie. Not to mention Aboo, our

OUR· GAZELLE.

escaped slave, we have the cook's family of pigeons, to which he has lately added a young dove, who, being tender, sleeps in the oven, which is a dangerous place for him. Then there is the companionable Kiki, whose nose is put out of joint by two rivals. One is an exquisite young gazelle which we bought yesterday, and which looks already reconciled to its new home. An Arab brought it at a tender age to a woman who has tamed it. It is the perfection of animal beauty, with its slender reedlike legs, its coat of golden brown, and its great lustrous eyes, which as last night it stared with admiringly at the full moon, returned orb for orb. It already licks our hands and kisses us, and eats willingly its doura, or, tied to a stake, crops the fresh grass of the bank. And now Ruskallah has just brought in a genuine young crocodile. He is in fine condition, and already snaps. He is but a baby, and was caught by a fisherman in a net. He is now lying in a huge bowl of water with his head just above the surface, apparently unconscious that his ancestors were deified in the temple above him. For their sake we shall call him Savak, for so was called the crocodile god of old. We trust to a moment of inspiration and our poetic souvenirs for a suitable name for the beloved gazelle.

Monday, 25th.

By breakfast time yesterday we were at the famous quarries of Silsilis. Across the river they had that same fresh look as of stone cut but yesterday, which I remember at Pentelicus, which reminds one of a Stilton cheese which the cheese-knife has economically pared away. This superior sandstone was as precious to the Egyptians as was Pentelicus to the Greeks; and if in Egypt there had been marble, its invitation to finish must have carried the sculpture forward farther than ever could the coarser sandstone. But it is best as it is; the world as much needs the severe impeccable outline of Egypt, its expression of abstract thought through form, as the more human, tenderer sculpture of Greece. Yet what a satisfactory picture did we not see in one of the tombs here; it needed nothing that Greece or Asia could have given it, complete in itself, and indeed the antitype of an episode of one of Raphael's most famous frescoes, in which the Pope enters, borne on his litter with the flabella above his head. Here was the original. Horus the king, not Horus the divinity—and he preceded all the Rameses, and this picture makes modern even Aboo Simbel—Horus seated, a lion by his side, the flabella borne aloft, while a trumpeter marshals forward the procession, and bound captives precede. Eugenio made a careful drawing of the group, which will be precious to him for the best art of Egypt is there. Close by this picture is another of Horus suckled by a goddess. The attitude and movement is identical with the group at Denderah;

of course the latter is a copy. Etiquette is the necessity of courts and religions. As a Spanish queen could not put on her night-gown unless the proper tire-woman were by, so a goddess can only suckle a hero after one formula. Doesn't modern manners retain something of this, even if it have discarded the starch of Brummel? In this same tomb-grotto are the squares and outlines of a far earlier artist than him of Kom Ombos. At this time the surface of the stone was prepared by a glaze or varnish, which retains the finest work uninjured.

There were niches in this grotto where small mutilated gods were seated.

The ancestral Yankee has a strain of blood which expresses itself here as it does with us by whittling. Here there is so little wood they take stone instead, but everywhere there are flourishes of the pen-knife. Stelæ and pigmy tombs are cut all about as in wantonness, and there are those great gashes, scoops of the knife, quite different from the look of the nibbling pick, which we have seen everywhere on the monuments; here they abound on the faces of the rock.

We did not cross the river to visit the great quarries, but gazed with deep respect at that mountain's brow, as we might upon that of some great artist, whence had issued such poems as Karnak and Medinet Haboo.

The only wind in our favour since we came down blew while Eugenio was sketching. But we rowed, and we drifted, and had the pleasure to see that at least it blew somebody good. With nobly swelling sails, and many abreast, ten dahabeahs came rustling by us, mid the chattering cross-fire of dragomen and sailors. All but one were English—if they meet General Maclellan's fleet, will there be a naval engagement?

Poor Mr. Todd had one, an encounter with an English boat in the very thunder of the Cataract. There were displayed abnormal tactics, and he was driven upon a rock, where his foe tried to secure him by a rope, but he bravely cut it and sailed away.

In the evening I took my gun and Arab, and wandered far along the shore in vague hope of sand-grouse or foxes. I got only a distant shot at a hawk, and came back by one of those sunsets which, after the blank lustre of Nubia, seems homelike. Here there are clouds and softness and endless lines of distance. The hum of the sakia is dead, and no more shall we see the lovely Nubian maiden — for we did really find her at last, with her gazelle-like timidity, her oily tresses, and her beautiful sky-blue lips.

The enchanter who turns so many gods and heroes into basalt and blackstone has removed his spell, and we breathe again the happy sunshine of Egypt. Later Rus- kallah tried the hill for foxes — vainly, and as soon as he returned, away went we to the tune of the rudder, which reminds us of the sakia we have lost.

This morning we saw the pylon of Edfoo's unrivalled temple, and when the adverse wind had tossed us about for an hour, we wished we had stopped. The lamp is swinging as gaily as does a lamp at sea, and we fondly speculate upon Mr. Bessemer and his horizontal cabin.

28th.

How lucky we are to have a current in our favour; without that we should never reach Cairo, for the breeze blows steadily against us, which, fortunately, is all gain for those going up. Not only that, but the conflicting wind and current make a little sea, which stimulates the peristaltic motion in many a dahabeah. Luckily sea-sickness is soon forgotten; and the romantic traveller tries to believe it never existed.

But after all what a bore the Nile must be to many of that herd of travellers who, driven from their firesides by the physician or fashion, utterly unprepared by study or reflection for interest to track the footsteps of the past, with no love of literature, no skill in sketching, secretly longing for the routine they have escaped, how can they often here fail to wish themselves well home again ? On Tuesday, without confessing it, we ourselves were secretly soured by the weary weather, and were glad to get out for a four mile stretch on foot to Esné. Dropping down the rapids, the *Rachel* followed us, and arrived just as we had fairly finished our coffee at one of the cafés of the bank. It was the same Esné we remember, looking with its right-angled houses like one of Poussin's towns, as we approached it. The ghawazees were there in swarms, with their ugly long striped calico dresses, and alas ! the flies we knew before under the bank had only said "*au revoir*," and awaited us. There was a file of dahabeahs, and among them acquaintances. From them we got home papers ; and how the flimsy cotton paper, the small pale type and the string of debilitated fun remind us that a democracy is not absolute perfection.

Fortunately that silence which the absence of letters inspires with terror seems to be innocent of calamity, and if they are well at home, have we not here the burden of a great grief? Our baby crocodile is dead! Savak mourns for it through all his palaces of mud, and we share his woe. We cannot guess which killed it, the coldness of the water in its pan, or the fatigue of its journey, head downward, in the hand of the Arab. At all events it presents the creature in a new light, not the unassailable tyrant of the river, but with sensibility, perhaps even sentiment, making his life precarious.

February 3d.

We reached Thebes the afternoon of the 29th, and it looked strangely familiar to us. The same dusty bank, the same consular flags floating above it, and the buried columns which give so much dignity to the little town. Alas! no letters. We are still thrust out into darkness and barbar-

R

ism, and not until we reach Asyoot are we to hear those dear bells, better than any fancied bells of the desert, which ring for us of home and affection.

Returning from the disappointing consul, I met Mariette Bey, and had a pleasant chat with him. He could not accept our invitation for dinner, suffering from indisposition. We spoke together of Caviglia, and he deplored the vandal of the dahabeah who still insists on defacing the old sculptures for the paltry satisfaction of possessing a bit of them. He has to hide his pretty things sometimes for years, as from naughty children. He has several *caches* now, and the tomb at Aboo Simbel opened this year was discovered three years ago. There is but one guardian appointed in Egypt, and he is stationed at Edfoo. It seems strange that the Khedive, so advanced in many things, should neglect to protect the temples, which, even as property, are daily growing in value. M. Mariette announced the arrival speedily of two royal personages, one the Duke of Mecklenburg-Schwerin. He invited me to offer for his boat my own place, and I said that to oblige Mariette Bey I would do it, but not otherwise. The other royal person, Prince Arthur of England, really came the next day, which the Duke did not, and our politeness was thrown away. The transit of Venus is as nothing compared to the transit of a prince, and by four in the afternoon of the 30th all Luxor was alive. As twilight approached the steamer was sighted, and then brighter burned the little lamps which spelled out in a rather Arabian way the Prince's name over the English consul's door, and more exultingly leaped about the three or four horsemen who were making believe play at the jereed ; and slowly through the staring crowd on the bank filtered the few loyal English here, who came to sun themselves in the brightness of royalty. Wishing to share in the general joy, we hung our boat with lanterns, and as the *Sybil* had a dinner-party, and for that was illuminated, we both were invited to send to the appreciative Prince the boat's name and our own. No English boat was as gay as were our two.

The *Clara* is here and two of General Maclellan's fleet, and we interchange visits. We compare our comforts and our troubles, ask after the condition of the pets, discuss if the Nile be or not a humbug, and exchange newspapers and news.

One poor fellow who had no dahabeah, but came in a Cook's party, paid us a visit. He was not very fond of the apparatus of Mr. Cook for happiness ; nor did he find it even cheap. There was little fellowship in the party, and their *table d' hôte* of temples, like that of their dinner, being taken in a herd, gave little individual satisfaction. He somewhat pathetically apologised for his liberty in calling, but he was glad to get beyond his beat, and comforted himself that, alone as he was, he could not have done better.

We gave a day to Karnak, and two days to the other side of the river, and then came away. Karnak persists in leaving an impression so terrible that familiarity does not blunt it. Elsewhere the ruins are intelligible, and even soothing in their quiet. Here the confusion which existed when they were whole destruction but confounds the more. There is no place so pathetic as this. One may call it awful to see thus doomed man's grandest expression of reverential worship; and it is like a nightmare to see pylons in half overthrow, which will not fall, and displaced blocks and slanted columns hanging above us as if to prolong the agony of our dream; and when, at the crumbling foot of the still upright columns, you push your cane, it comes away red as with blood from the disorganised sandstone. I made the circuit of the ruins, and stretched away to a far pylon, as if one were clambering from a ruined St. Paul's to a ruined Westminster Abbey, so vast is the interval, and I found at each step the earth making confession of the greatness it had lost. From one point I counted seven pylons, and for what completeness and beauty of architecture each stood I well knew.

We revisited each point that had struck us before, but found them well branded into our memory, vague but deep, and a second sight could add but little to the impression. If there is exultation in the first aspect of so much grandeur, melancholy replaces it now ; a sense of uneasiness, pathetic pity, and finally something of despair, haunts us, and will for ever, as we think how impotent and futile is man's struggle with the victorious forces of Nature.

At Medinet Haboo we were fresh, which before we were not, and the long procession, the mystic boats, the mighty gods, and calm Rameses still slaughtering his foes, had their lines cut into the smooth morning polish of our minds, as were they into the enduring sandstone. I drew over again the same characteristic barbarian

prisoner, and could have drawn one by
one every wall, so inviting it was.
Eugenio, reckless even of lunch, lost himself in some sculptured procession, material
for his great picture of the Fête of the Rising of the Nile; and long after we were
resting our weary limbs at home, he, pencil
in hand, was still marching down that long
procession of the years. We did not visit
the Memnonium again, but it was compen-
sated by a visit to a little temple close to
the hills, and built on terraces. There the
beauty of the stone had invited the whole
skill of the artist, and the figures had a
finish and charm which perhaps place it
among Egypt's best things.

Saturday evening the American consul
made up a party to see the ghawazee girls.
They were four in number, backed by a
few friends and a band of music. The
consul looked on sedately while smoking,
as though he had been in church. It was
the same thing as before; the same raised
arms, and all the *tremblement*, as the

French say—a quivering motion from the hips downward, but not so well done as we had seen at Asyoot. For this and other civilities I was given to understand the worthy consul expected a backsheesh, I in return receiving antiquities; so I parted with my useless pistol, which will add its mite to the uproar by which dahabeahs are welcomed.

Monday night we dropped down the river to visit early the next day the tombs of the Kings. Nor was a living prince wanting there to do them honour, for we found Prince Arthur before us. His suite were busy taking paper impressions, and we had our pick from the surplus. We were all ardour to see these tombs, the finest in Egypt. They impress all, and we had read Miss Martineau's eloquent flights, and Mariette's and Lepsius's more learned pages, till perhaps they were the one thing we most wished to see.

Nothing scenically could be more grandly appropriate than the approach. There is

through all Egypt a faint flavour of mummy
in the air ; it seems to fly in the dry dust-
cloud, and we perceive it in the brown rai-
ments of peasants, which look often so like
mummy-cloths. It hangs around a dahabeah, in the blue necklaces we purchase,
and indeed the land is one sublime charnel-
house, saved only from mournfulness by
the ever fertilising river of life which passes
through it. Life and death here are indeed
in excess, and in perpetual contrast. Nowhere is the sentiment of life, its returning
bloom and freshness, so felt as here ; and
this recurring fertility seems as that of
earth's dawn, while the mountains are haggard around it with the generations gone.
And as we moved up the winding valley
nearer to the tombs, the vast mountain
vertebrae and bones of limestone seemed
in their death but the precursors to those
millions they entombed. We noticed that
the limestone was ribbed with flint nodules,
itself of a delicacy like that of whetstone,
while the strange rounded tops, towering

like swathed and crumbling giants, were black with the broken flint.

This Journal cannot pretend to describe in detail these majestic burial-places which we could so partially examine. There is a fatigue of the mind more searching than that of the body, and when, like a full sponge, it has enough, it turns wearily away from what it can no longer enjoy. Oh, that one but had these tombs at one's door, to return again and again and master each hidden meaning and enjoy each brilliant sculpture.

The first tomb we visited was Belzoni's. The peasants, noticing the rain's infiltration through a crevice, and he finding the rock hollow, a few sturdy pushes with a palm trunk lay open to him a tomb unvisited since the artist sealed its mouth. We deeply sympathised with his enthusiasm, which must have been as great as a human brain could bear. Everything was then in its place as when left; but now, in spite of the splendid fulness of beauty which remains, Howadgi and Arab have been more deadly enemies than the centuries to what should have been sacred to any one who respects the sanctity of death.

In this as in the other tombs, we descended by an inclined plane to horizontal walls, passing by lofty doors from one to the other, with lateral chambers seven or eight in number, and each square foot of surface was either word or picture. How can one recall these striking things, which, as wave chases wave, drive from the eye and the memory each succeeding impression ? But one terrible picture, the most impressive of its kind I ever saw, can never be effaced. It was a solitary figure standing on a platform. It had ascended while the forty-two judges were watching it, awed, but hopeful, before Osiris, who was to absolve or condemn it. It was the silhouette merely of a man. It might stand for any human soul ; the haughtiest king, the poorest slave, must so look when waiting the judgment of his God. But while

this came up to all that Christianity demands of grandeur for the final scene, these
tombs, like all others in Egypt, have a
cheerfulness their solemn temples want.
With the old Egyptians death is always
life—life continued under new conditions,
—yet little unlike to this.   They were not
ashamed of a creed like that of the Indian
who hoped—

"Admitted to that equal sky,
   His faithful dog should bear him company."

And here were those greyhounds, just like
ours, which we have heard have been mistaken for jackals in the head of Anubis.
Yet the dog Anubis of the death-boats, so
terribly impressive in his rigid attitude,
seems no greyhound, but rather a mastiff.
One chamber was dedicated to instruments
of war.   There was the whole equipment
of a warrior, his helmet, his corselet—like
that of the sculptures — his sword, short
and hollow in the handle, like the modern
Egyptian sword, and the blue of its blade,

as well as of all other objects which might be steel, was so evidently steel that we were delighted to have our minds on this point at rest for ever.

These swords, so painted, are in the tomb of Sethi I., father of the Great Rameses, and probably steel had been known in Egypt for ages before. Now we can understand the cutting of the hieroglyphics, the shaping of the stones. All that remains to confound us is the transport of the enormous blocks. That we know to have been done by huge rafts, as the pictures show, for even the Colossi were so conveyed.

Next to the warrior's chamber was one full of boats, which had the single square sail cut up into coloured checks, and often wearing on its prow the garlands we had seen on the death-boats. Elsewhere we saw wheat, fresh as last year's, and gathered by a sickle identical with our own. In fact it is but too plain that the whole machinery of civilisation has been thought out at some remote time. For ourselves, we have only our new inventions.   Even the plough was identical with those now working the plain below.

In Bruce's tomb we saw the famous harper, in fact two harpers, with harps which, for elegance, Erard might envy.   And again, the lateral chambers, fresh in their colours, overflowed with what seemed the life of yesterday. Snakes, spotted and barred, of various colours, sometimes many-headed, glided along the walls, and at times wound about throngs of figures, as the emblem of eternity.   And there was the incredible female figure stretching along the whole ceiling, like some Majilton of the dead, grotesquely comic, though taken seriously, no doubt, by the men of old.   And we must protest, once for all, against the idea that the old Egyptians were mournful in their austerity.   Their religion was a ceremonial religion of *fêtes* and processions, whose root sprang from the grandest conceptions of the forces of Nature and man's obligation.   These ceremonies were confined to king and priesthood; the people were not even admitted within the temple; but if this religion shut itself within rigid formulas, it did not crush the Egyptian spirit. There breathes everywhere from these pictures of the olden life a happiness and cheer which we sadly miss in the churchyards of the Christian. Egypt deified the forces of nature; connected them, as in Osiris, with the sentiment of conscience; or, as in Athor, the sentiment of harmony; and who of us shall say them nay to conceptions which have proved themselves as immortal as are their sculptured emblems on these walls?

Though they were a reverential people, their sensibility to the ornamental and useful arts was exquisite, and their prosperity and national life lasted longer than that of any nation we know.

As of late the river has been windless, we get on famously. With rowing we make as much as four miles an hour, equal to good speed with the sail going up. I am glad to find that each party gets to love its Arab crew, as we certainly do ours. They are like children with something of a man's strength, and very willing and patient. Without much power of communication with them, they slowly individualise themselves, and we learn to distinguish Achmed from Abdallah, as if we had known them long. They smile when we do, and echo our cries of confidence and cheer, and when they get hurt, as they often do, they come very meekly to the lady physician of the boat, and they will take unflinchingly from her such a dose of castor-oil as should upset a regiment. To be sure, like children, they will unwind the lint from their wounds, and irritate them when told not to, like naughty boys. They have at least one vice, though as to that there are temperance men among them, and the foul fume of their hasheesh reaches us at times on the upper deck. But what a thing it is to have no drunkard's blood among them. Their characters could not keep their sunshine if they had ; the curse of the North is this sad substitute for sunshine, souring the temper, making sullen or ferocious wretches of honest people, and alike a difficulty for priest and statesman to deal with. Our sailors' oars clang through the night, and we smite the sounding furrows, as did Ulysses, trying to learn more of men and cities.

We reached Kenneh, with temptations on both sides of the river ; we refused one, and kept all our strength for the famous temple of Denderah. It was hardly more than a mile's trot to the ruins, and my donkey was not only sure-footed, but for the first time I had long stirrups. The traveller in Egypt who does not love the donkey is to be pitied. It is at home here, and looks it. It is not so very far hence that Lepsius saw him in his native wilds, the free untamed ass of the desert. When caught, he tells us that it is long before they submit to man ; they retain

S

something of that unconquered savageness
which is still the birthright of their poetic
brother the zebra, which never bears a
saddle.   The Egyptian donkey is smaller
than his English cousin, less shaggy in his
coat, and with smaller head.   There is a
different look in his eye, something of that
velvet softness which makes the difference
between the Jew of Smyrna and of London.   Our dear gazelle has it in its pure
perfection, and each of her lake-like eyes
has never imaged anything narrower than
the boundless desert and the limitless
heaven above it.   There is a half smile
always on the donkey's face here, and his
little wiry legs over their delicate hoofs at
times carry weights incredible to us.   I see
often some huge Arab, perhaps with a lap-
ful of parcels, suddenly melt away and
become a brown spot on the ground.   I
myself have been tumbled into the sand
within a few days, and neither I nor the
donkey were the worse for it.   But oh, for
Mr. Bergh of New York !   He could do a

good work in Egypt, where it is the wicked custom of the donkey driver to establish a raw on the back behind, which he perpetually prods with a little stick. Civilisation does this, for in Nubia we did not see it. Let us hope that for this the donkey feels some consolation in the superb runners of Cairo, who, like birds of bright plumage, fly along the streets, their flowing sleeves tied up behind, in front their breasts one blaze of crimson and gold. What a dear, graceful, swiftly running softly smiling one we had at Cairo, and how we all loved him! And Mr. Darwin could still count some bars of the zebra on these subjected asses. When he is well cared for, he is of lofty stature, wears gorgeous housings, and is generally of a pretty mouse colour; his coat fancifully trimmed with the scissors, his tail and mane artistically notched. What a pity we cannot manage to breed such a race in America.

In three quarters of an hour we were at

the temple. Though this is Ptolemaic work, it is counted among the great treasures of Egypt, for the whole of the old religion seems written out on it, as in a missal. All the new ideas of Platonic Christianity were infused into the old religion, till we may say that here Egypt and Judea give each other the hand. Down in the crypts, up on the uninjured terrace (where nestle two little temples, and to which one ascends on either side by the longest and easiest staircase we ever saw), everywhere is spelled out in hieroglyphics the mighty story. The temple is like a madrepore or brain coral, so wrought is it. The ceilings are full of new and significant astronomical devices, but too blackened to be fairly seen ; these continue the tale, and lovely Athor, the goddess whose dress was beauty, whose movement was sweetness and harmony, presides here.

This and Edfoo are the two perfect temples of Egypt, and for a wonder, though Ptolemaic, its columns are as heavy as those

of the olden time. Nowhere is the sur-
rounding wall of unburnt brick, which shut
out the crowd, so perfect and intelligible as
here. Though the sculptures are full of
meaning, of course they have little beauty,
the hand of Rome had neither the genuineness nor the cunning that wrought the
true sculptures of Egypt.

Not far from the large temple is a small
one, whose presiding god till lately has
been disputed. The funny little monster,
plainly enough carved, was thought to be
Typho, but as there is a long row of figures,
each on its knee dandling a child, it seemed
merely repetitions of Athor and her baby.
A pleasanter interpretation was sought.
The god is now found to be Bes,——one of
mirth and frolic, and well suited to a
nursery. It is a comfort to find some-
where a temple erected to that force in
human nature which enables us to bear
the tragedy of life, and distinguishes man
from the animals. Christianity has failed
to provide any shrine for mirth, which God

sent in pity to his children—but condemns it as a mistake, and anticipating hypocrisy, brands with disgrace one of the champions of truth and liberty.

Feb. 5th.

The Journal gains if the voyage loses. For two days a wind which shakes the souls within us detains the boat, but gives us time for long inland explorations. Yesterday in our shell-boat Ruskallah and I went for ducks and geese.   Delightful was the spin, multitudinous the geese, pleasant the cautious approach across the cleanly sand-bar, but we fired from too far for success, and came back skirting the bank to allow pigeons and sic-sacs to come hopping up to our oars unmolested, while a great whirl of sand enveloped our dahabeah, and drove it into harbour at Dishneh.   To-day our exploration carried Eugenio to the top of the limestone mountain with difficulty, while we, skirting its base, admired where the limestone became cretaceous, the belts

of yellow and white being very striking. Ruskallah brought from his walk huge fossil oysters, and Eugenio crystals and jasper. Alas, for Abydus and the grave of Osiris! it escapes us, and our time for such delights is short.

These windy grey days are not without their compensation; they give us exquisite sunsets. Last night's the Journal tries to remember by this record.

A SUNSET.

Past emerald plains and furrowed mountains old,
Whose violet gorges snare the wandering eye,
The pillared palms day's dying embers hold,
Like shafts of bronze against the crimson sky,
And every cloud mirrors its rosy fold
In tremulous waves which blush and wander by—
We float, and feel the magic penetrate,
Till all our soul is coloured by the hues,
Making a heaven of earth, till, satiate
With splendour, we forego the use
Of speech, and reverently wait
While fades the glory with the falling dews,
And darkness seals for memory each gleam,
Happy to know it was not all a dream.

February 7th.

For the very important visit to Abydus—
that exquisite ruin of the best day, near
which M. Mariette even concedes the
tomb of Osiris may be, buried under those
who came from all parts of Egypt to lie
near him, and in which is the famous list of
kings, seventy-six in number, beginning
with the fabulous Menes and ending with
Sethi I., who built this temple—the gods
kindly gave us most perfect weather. The
day was a long delight, for, well rested
from the fatigue of our visit to the Tombs
of the Kings, we were ready for the seven
mile trot to Abydus. We were not un-
lucky in our donkeys ; there was no wind,
the road was good, and, above all, there was
in the air that faint breath of the spring,
which for the first time we had felt a few
days before. That breath unlooses something of longing and hope in the soul of
man, and his body shares with the earth
that tremor of content when winter, how-

ever faint its load, passes away. The fields of wheat and lupin, which we had left so young, were now breast high, and the scent of the lupin, pleasantly mingled with the nameless odours which came from these rich fields, (for this country is prosperous), and great herds of sheep nibbling at the fringe of the lupins, noble bullocks and cows, gave a patriarchal air to the landscape. Many a lordly Jacob resting on his staff seemed with content overlooking his vast possessions. Three towns dotted our way, and from each came the gathering yell of Egypt's *gamin*, and their willing train followed at our heels, all proclaiming that though religions and dynasties may pass, one faith survives, and these were its followers, and the god's name they for ever shouted, which village passes on to village, and river bank to river bank, and it is " backsheesh." The sight of the howadgi, and the conviction of his worship of false gods, causes them more exultingly to proclaim for ever their own. The silent peasant in the fields, women at their water-jars, the pensive traveller on the camel's back, babies in arms, at the sight of the howadgi defiantly pronounce the name of him whom they adore.

A dozen beautiful sand-grouse within easy shot seemed to know that Paolo had not brought my gun, which I did not. Our dinner of to-morrow triumphantly escaped the dish, and my scolding had to be kept back till I returned. When there, I found our Arab guard had refused to take it, fearing he might injure it, and consequently suffer.

We were two hours in getting to the base of the cliffs where Abydus lies. It is difficult to speak without undue enthusiasm of the beauty of this temple. The best sculptures in it are cut in the creamy lime-stone, so close and fine that it equals marble. Indeed, while the grain is nearly as close, the colour is far better—quite a perfect tint for sculpture. There is no need here of that superposed surface which coarser stone demands. Time has not touched it, and the execution, finished as if on ivory in many places, is absolutely as when it left the workman's hands. The blocks of the roof and the columns are made of the coarser and redder limestone, but the walls everywhere are of this beautiful material. The character of the sculpture has that indescribable something which we find in the Parthenon. A sense of something superior to human work, an ease, and at the same time a finish, a bloom of youth and of earth's morning, yet with the maturity of skill and thought, make such masterpieces the high-water mark of man's achievement and precious for ever.

Eugenio took as many paper impressions as he could, and they lie now in his room, retaining even in that shape the noble sweetness of those beautiful faces. There is no higher type of Egyptian beauty than here. The full smiling mouth, the delicately arched nose, ears perfectly executed, and a form of head which we again and

again notice to be of the best Caucasian
type.

There is much more accurate modelling
than when, later, art was but an imitative
formula. The bones of the knee are
indicated, the hands expand and grasp
naturally, the muscles are correctly marked,
and the feet sometimes bent with a true
action of the toes, though large, are beautiful. There is nothing of that rigidity
anywhere which we popularly ascribe
to Egyptian art. These were the fresh
natural originals, and they who came afterwards, in the forms as probably in their
worship, made their creed as well as their
art a formula and slavish imitation. It
was vexatious to find that M. Mariette had
buried his treasure—yet who had a better
right, as he found it? The tablet of the kings
is thus saved from the dangerous admiration
of the howadgi. No doubt he expects a
guardian to be appointed, and then this
precious thing will be shown to all. But
two tablets of cartouches, one of sixty and

one of more than eighty kings, are visible
in two of the chambers. The savants tell us
that the meaning of this temple is obscure.
It was built conjointly by Sethi and his
son Rameses. Rameses is figured many
times as being suckled, and the figure of his
father stretched in death is very impressive.
Sethi, whose tomb is called Belzoni's,
was buried in the alabaster sarcophagus
found there, and now is in the Soane
Museum in London, and Sethi's own body
was found in it. Well may Hamlet moralise
upon the fate of kings and conquerors.
The figures in this temple are tall, nor are
those executed for his son Rameses when
in outline, short, but the Colossi have not
the same proportion. Probably it was
thought that a certain sturdiness and bulk
was the most important thing in a colossal
figure. Instead of an adytum there are
seven chambers at the temple's end.
These have the most beautiful sculpture,
and in each, at the farther wall, what looks
like a double door with rich carving above

it, is sculptured. They were not doors, and were never opened, but an ornament representing a bamboo curtain rolled up, precisely like our own, seems to show that they figured windows or doors in stone. We have seen nothing like them in any other temple.

As the tomb of Osiris is only conjectured, and its site a heap of rubbish, we did not visit it, but saving our donkeys for the long way back, left to imagination the thought of that great presence which M. Mariette avers may yet prove a reality.

Our cup running over with content, we returned through the beautiful fields—the wheat extending as far as the eye could reach, and the delicate freshness of receding day acting like a tonic to our weary muscles. And when is a cup of tea more of an elixir than when after such well earned fatigue, we slowly sip it on our divan — the dear, fadeless pictures still floating before our eyes, and a memory lodged in the heart which makes such a day golden among the many ?

8th.

For the last two days we have been the prey of circumstance, making twenty-five miles in all, and unable often to proceed. In spite of rowing, just now we have been forcibly driven against a bank by an eddy, and for our amusement could only watch some hundred people who poured a basket-ful of earth at a time upon a dyke where this same eddy had forced itself through and drowned the plain. We asked them what they got for their work, and they replied : "Nothing! and are lucky if what we have is not taken from us besides." A lovely government and a patient people, and such they have been from the dawn of time !

This morning at Ihkmeen we had a charming walk through the town, visiting the bazaar and making sketches of a street, above which rose a lovely minaret.

Eugenio purchased a superb rug, and I had the common wooden bolt, which shuts every door here, explained to me. It is kept in place by a number of nails which serve as wards, and which a notched stick unfastens. We sketched from the boat a most picturesque blind beggar, who would serve perfectly an artist as a study for the blind Bartimæus.

While in the bazaar, in contrast with his rags, we saw merchants in crimson and gold flashing into the sunlight like Chinese pheasants. It is dreadful hereabouts to read Murray, for he tells long stories of tombs and temples everywhere, which we cannot contrive to see. It is the punishment of Tantalus to read of pictures we shall never see, hidden in the golden hills which invite us from town to town.

Our pets thrive wonderfully. Poor Aboo Simbel is like a re-creation from death. Well fed and in European clothes, every day his look is cheerfuller, and now he even laughs. When we first got him, he was so weak and discouraged by the daily whippings he got for falling asleep at the sakia, that he could but drag one leg after the other. Yesterday the lordly koorbash was given him to protect the farm-yard and the lovely gazelle from the crowd, and when an Arab tried to seduce him from his allegiance to us, he fell to and lashed the tempter. His hands, unaccustomed to delicate work, are curiously clumsy, and he carries a cup of coffee as if it were a red-hot coal. But sweeping he manages well, and can now see his face in the boots he polishes, which shine in ebon rivalry of each other. The little dove daily grows in plumpness, and seems to have no dread of the kitchen fire ; the pigeons roost in a line upon our fallen yard, in friendly society with fluttering hundreds of nimble sparrows who come and go. So plentiful are they, they sometimes make on a rope an unbroken line for many yards, and the saucy things coolly steal the doura of the turkeys before their very eyes. These

T

turkeys seem sometimes to speculate upon
their future fate, and the other day, when
the smiling Nubian came to take the last
one from its coop, it seemed to know
whither its brothers had gone, and fiercely
pecked his hand. The dear gazelle is
hourly more precious in our eyes. She
relishes her grass and doura, and it is
pleasant to see her satisfaction when nibbling the grass on the bank, for we take her
out every day when we stop, and sometimes
Aboo gives her little runs for exercise.

I do not know what secret glamour Kiki has, but we think there never was such
a cat. The living topaz of its eyes flashes
daily more brightly, and daily do the
beautiful hairs of its coat come out more
vividly. It is rapidly passing, as its round
waist shows, to the maturity of cathood, but
it seems fondly to try and make the most
of what kitten there is left. Our little
cabin is no fit scope for its agility, and it
bounds from side to side as does a squirrel
in its cage. Unfortunately its too great

genius for locomotion in furtive passages reluctantly forces us to keep it a prisoner at night. The other day, being carelessly put where the butter of the sailors was, of course it ate it, and when whipped by them must have marvelled at the unfairness of such a sequence. Not long since, in attempting to reach bait on a fish-hook, it got hooked itself, and though now well, it was touching to see it try to rub away the pain from the outside.

There are several places about here which have a bad reputation, and we have even had a couple of guards twice appointed to watch over us. One night a gipsy Bedawee came from a tent near by, with a funny little yellow dog, just the dog for a gipsy, and when we talked of buying him, he said : " You may have him for nothing, for what can I do with money." I even gave him a two piastre piece, and he returned it. He carried, dangling from his waist, a huge curved sword whose scabbard was half made of snake skin.

Nor are these dangerous fellows always only problematical criminals. Eugenio returned delighted with his sketch, but shocked with what he had seen in the market-place. A fellah was hanging there on a gibbet since the morning. The year before he had stolen melons, and had killed four of the police, three outside and one inside his prison, in desperation. It was interesting to notice that his arms were held by oval wooden gyves, such as confined the arms of the prisoners of Rameses; a common chain confined his ankles.

With the exception of "taib," "battal" and "ketir" our conversation with our Arabs on excursions is mostly confined to unintelligible exclamations. These seem to give partial satisfaction, and we mutually repeat the last word of each other's sentences. If we only could talk Arabic how much might we not learn of the lives and habits of these clever fellows. What they really think on any matter we know as little as when we made their acquaintance. Thus familiarity does not take away the vague poetry which to us surrounds the life of the Arab. They sleep in the moonlight and the wind, always covering the face, wrapped in their long brown cloaks, yet ready at a hint to rise, and sitting on their sheepskins, which once held our by-gone dinners, row through long hours of the night. Comparing ourselves with others, we find we are peculiarly lucky in the musical powers of our crew. We like to hear their refrain during the watches of the night, and the tunes, half merry and half melancholy, with which they fill their leisure evenings.

Such music is like the wash of the waves against our boat, the far heard moan of the camel, or the sakia's wail ; something which is borrowed from the rythmical movement of natural sounds, and seems but the river singing over its work.

When they sing at night, or jabber in the daytime, and we ask what the words mean, we are always told it is something about love, which only makes it all sound the more romantic.   And romance will not leave their swelling, sonorous Arabic names, though to them they may sound as common as John or Thomas.   After hearing in rich tones such names as Abdallah, Achmed, Fatma, we sometimes smile when looking over a list of odd London names which we collected last spring, mostly from signs, as we glanced on either side from our hansom.   Here are some of them.   They certainly do not breathe of Arabia, but of the prosier North :—

William Cutbush, E. Waterer, gardeners.
Whips, sold by E. Whippey.
Miss Heaven, Mr. Hell.
Mr. Gotobed.
Rev. Arthur Gabbell.
Mrs. Howgiggle.
August Toupet, coiffeur.
Waukenphast, boots, 25 Pall Mall.
A. Jolly, priest.

T. A. Dollar.

Tagus Shout, jeweller.

Mr. Green Sugars.

Mrs. Backhouse.

Miss Bairnsfather.

Mr. Death, jeweller.

Mr. Duck, Mr. Drake, Mr. Pease, Leeds, Upper Head Row.

William Dear.

W. Spittle.

W. Toogood, seedsman to the Queen.

Mr. Self.

E. Bonfellow.

Mr. Bizzle.

Mr. Pinch, shoemaker.

Mr. Coward.

Mr. Stab, surgeon.

Dr. E. R. Kill.

Mrs. Yungfleisch.

Mr. Grub, farmer.

Signor Goldfinger, Milan.

M. A. d'Aujourdhui, lithographer, Shaffhausen.

Friday, Feb. 12th.

On the morning of the 10th we reached Asyoot. It shone to us with a brightness which not even the Egyptian sky could give—the brightness of home—for here we swept into our dahabeah a whole harvest of letters, to be slowly enjoyed, as in a luxurious dream, upon our divan, while the tinkle at our bow swelled for us till it seemed the grander music of the Atlantic.

How our thoughts, threading space and mixing with those of the dear writers', laughed to scorn the cold iron of the wire beside us. This hunger of affection which had been starved so long, now satiated, showed itself in every face with a mild lambency. Nor were the letters needed to make Asyoot to us the loveliest town in Egypt. Its broad approach under flaring plane-trees, and its many minarets contribute to this. Only the larger towns in Egypt have minarets. Their beauty, as ornaments to the town, far exceeds what can be claimed for our steeples. They are just the right size, not ambitious to soar beyond reach, and the detail of their filigree work and balconies, always different, gives each one a character by itself. But they are silent save when the human cry to prayer is heard above their walls ; no tumult of joyous acclaim shows they share in the town's festivities, and no brazen heart-beat of devout emotion partakes of the Sunday's worship. But for a city which is not quite on a dead level, no structure can rival the dome, under which homes seem to nestle as beneath protecting wings. The sky-line of the dome alone is important, nor should it be ambitious of too vast a swell. Though for the reason, not only of its beauty and grandeur, but its solitariness amid the level wastes, is St. Peter's dome unrivalled, yet the dome of the State House of Boston, as seen from Brookline or Cambridge, satisfies the mind, and crowns the city as could neither spire nor minaret. The glory of Con-

stantinople is that there dome and minaret
uniting to carry up to heaven as with
flame, the loveliness of both, make a city
which, seated upon the waters, and towering
with stalactite shafts and ivory curves, the
memory of the eye can never forget.

Our consul at Asyoot in his pretty house,
and more like a European than any other
consul we have here met, gave us our letters,
and seeing our looks of wonder at so long
forgotten a thing as the calèche before his
door, offered to give us a drive in it, which
we would have accepted but that time
pressed. Feeling the hours of our journey
numbered, and determined not to lose the
tomb of the Colossus near Antinoë, we
arrived there in the lovely serene afternoon,
but too late to attempt it before dark, so
we contented ourselves with sauntering
past the palms to the little village of
E' Dayi é Nakhl. This, like so many here,
lies with its cubes of brown upon the arid
earth of the same colour, and whence the
green wave of the plain has receded like

water. Turning to the left, just as
that mysterious pensiveness which night
brings into the face of Egypt, put it and
our thoughts into harmony, we paused
upon the mounds of Antinoë. Like
billows which have gone over the city are
the wave-like mounds which now only stand
for it, but the immortal spark survives ; for
neither time, which has made dust of the
royal Friend and his devoted Lover, nor
the vanishing of the commemorative city,
can quench the glow of sympathy in us all
as we think of such devotedness and such
affection "in the fierce light which beats
upon a throne." They who admire the
languid beauty of Antinous in the Roman
galleries should remember that behind that
softness was an unselfishness which caresses
and fortune could not spoil.

ANTINOUS.

Even nigh the golden furnace of a throne,
Flower-like thy loyalty and noble heart
Could live unwithered, and thy better part
The canker of low selfishness disown,

Losing itself hid in another's love.
And when commanding Fate said " for thy friend,
Give what he prizes most," all fear above,
Or thought that death such intercourse should end,
Thy life thou gavest like some common thing ;
Shaming all else, and never to forget
The place of sacrifice, the lonely King
Beside the fatal wave a city set
Commemorative, which ruin but endears,
And thy name lives there whispered through our tears.

The next morning we were in saddle betimes, and much enjoyed our donkey-ride. Round the shoulder of a hill, past the quarries which furnish lime to the government, we found the celebrated tomb. Not only here, but in so many places along the river, the frowning cliffs are pierced with square holes, making them look, as I imagine Gibraltar to look, which is so punctured, for artillery.

But before we entered the tomb (for there is but one of real interest here) we satiated ourselves with the superb view. We had not looked down on the valley from so commanding a point, and the

curves of the river, with its glimmering
sand-bars and boat sails, like birds' wings
dividing the green, till its intensity became
opaline, and the horizon cliffs, like ribs of
gold above the river ; and higher than all
a sky, across whose purity floated the
black smoke=wreaths of Minieh, as in these,
our modern days, ignoble labour can sully
the poetry of the past.

Then we turned into the spacious rooms,
for such they are, so clean, so dry, so
shapely, that a little furniture only is wanting to transform such a tomb into an
elegant habitation. We studied the Colossus picture, which is the frontispiece to
Wilkinson's book, with great satisfaction.
Though the figures at the rope are somewhat injured, the Colossus itself, and the
little fellow who keeps time on his knee by
clapping hands, are quite perfect. Of
course the Colossus was the statue of the
Egyptian gentleman who owned the tomb.
His beard shows him to be a private
person. In the tomb, also, were hunting

and agricultural scenes—scenes of the chase, where a gigantic figure, with bended bow, drove before him flocks of antelopes and gazelles, and what looked like a compact body of ostriches or cranes, one could not quite be sure which. So this gentleman was probably a sporting parson, and the English having perpetuated the race would contemplate it with satisfaction.

Among the animals, with delight I recognised our beloved donkey, which I have seen on no wall before. He had the same look of cheerful patience and deliberate philosophy which we see in him now. The ceiling was blue, fretted with stars. Below was a kind of balustrade of bright clear colours, and in form like our own.

Besides loving sport the buried man must have been a great lover of good things. Geese and ducks were hanging about in clusters, plump, and inviting the spit. Clergymen even now have been known to be of his opinion on this matter.

Most of the old Egyptians are coloured

red, and it was curious to notice that the disfiguring Coptic crosses were of exactly the same tint. When one of these crosses is well planted over a beautiful figure, it seems to consider itself a successful religious argument. "Get out of this!" cries in turn each iconoclast, till science now, with its saucy smile, cries "Get out all of you!" Why has not somebody rehabilitated Domitian as some one has Nero? We are getting a tenderer feeling for him daily, and knowing the fly of Egypt, we can but sympathise with his boyish zeal which gave them no mercy, and knowing the fury of the Copt, we must pardon his persecution of the Christians.

And as martyrs are the seeds of the church, he may be praised for trying to sow for the future harvest as widely as he could.

And yet, when upon the banks of the Tiber, one contemplates the beautiful African marble, and sees everywhere cut in an oval DOMITIANUS; and when the fortunate Baron Visconti can tell you that this stone was wrought, perhaps this name cut, by the early Christians who were exiled to mines and quarries, a flush of indignation must take the place of all this pleasant irony.

The same day we dropped down the river, for the first time since Assouan using our sail, and had the whole afternoon for Beni Hassan. All Wilkinson is there. Like some learned jackal he has sucked the marrow of these bones. Since his time, degradation of tint and outline has gone on terribly fast, and how fortunate it is that he has secured for us in time so much that is valuable. It would be supererogatory to try to glean in his footsteps, and folly to repeat what he has anticipated.

The famous tombs whose pictures he has copied are among many others, all of which we entered, sometimes finding on the farther wall endless groups of wrestlers in every conceivable attitude, but generally otherwise without paintings. These wrestlers suggest the funeral games of the Greeks, and lines of Homer sing a vague *refrain* in the memory. In some of the tombs, these wrestling figures extend across a wall at least twenty-five feet long, and there are seven or eight rows of them. These tombs are very spacious ; they are sustained by columns from two to twelve in number. The Doric column abounds, but certain slender shafts are purely Egyptian.

These halls of death are but ante-chambers ; there is always a slanting pass-age downward from them to the real tomb. Not only did not corruption invade them, but in them is no hint of the lugubrious images by which we vulgarise the great transition. Still the fowler snares—still the fisherman draws his net—still before him the hunter drives his prey—still, on every side, waves the wheat, and life retains its pomp and cheer. No hiatus in life is acknowledged; wherefore, then, should man try to shroud in gloom the precipice in which he refuses to believe ? Christianity

U

might have learned much of serene cheer, from what it despised as pagan.

The method of interment has much to do with the associations which accompany death.   As the Jews buried their dead in the earth, thoughts of corruption and the worm were forced upon them ; but in these high aerial chambers, dressed and perfumed for death as for a banquet, a kind of immortality mocked at dissolution, and from the walls around still breathed a life which could not be surrendered.

The Christians brought from Judea burial in the earth, and even now the earlier Roman idea, which distributes to the air man's poor remains, is the thought of many who sicken at the festering grave-yards of overcrowded Europe.

Sunday, 14th.

Sunday has come upon us unawares, for there is nothing here to mark the day. But though service on the Nile may be irregular or foregone, we comfort ourselves in knowing that never did we go so often to church. Yet, indeed, only to the temples of that venerable Mother Church which, in some sense, all later ones she can call her children. And no sermon or ritual service in chapel or cathedral can so sting the mind with ineffable longings to know the truth—can plumb with so deep a line the dark places of the soul as do these pathetic, voiceless fanes of an extinct belief.

We awoke to-day in a whirlwind. The lofty cliffs of light ochre opposite to us were veiled, and above them the sun splintered his rays like broken arrows against such bastions of clouds as before we have not seen. Soon the cliffs were lost to view, and a gale tore the tender waters of the Nile into shapes which only befit the sea. Luckily we were already against the bank, which we took last evening with a heavy thump, which must have come from a hidden rock.

As it is impossible to go on with such a wind, though favourable, and the reis wishes to bake bread for his men, Eugenio and I, to fill the time up, visited the sugar factory of Magada.

The superintendent kindly showed us all over it. We saw the rollers which chew the juice of the cane, as does everybody here, and the refuse heaped in the court behind, which still is valuable as fuel. We saw the slow chemistry by which the liquid is played with through vats and boilers till the smell we know so well, and which the drunkard loves, announced that rum was not far off; we saw the solemn dusky line of prodigious hogsheads in which the spirit is entombed—we saw a sugar sweeter and browner than any I ever saw before—and, finally, a coarse white sugar, to reach which all these wheels had been put in motion.

The superintendent kindly answered a few questions also. He told me the engineers and skilled workmen got as much as forty pounds a month, but that the common Arab workman had five piastres, equal to a shilling a day—certainly not bad wages for Egypt. The total quantity of sugar a-day is a thousand caritars, equal to a hundred thousand pounds per diem. There are twenty-two of these sugar-mills, and they are all owned by the Khedive. Since we have descended to statistics, we will mention the following :—

Our journey up and down the river is 1635 miles.

We have bought and eaten between forty and fifty sheep and five hundred chickens. The cabin has consumed four hundred, and Ruskallah is now seeing the end of seventeen hundred cigars — so insatiable is the Arab and his backsheesh. Two hundred bottles of wine and spirits have disappeared.

Our crew consists of twelve men and the reis, and our Nubian slave Aboo, the dragoman, the cook, the waiter, and ourselves make twenty-one. As the crew live on a kind of bread soup seasoned with lentils, and do not drink wine, the consumption of this is confined to the cabin. To be sure, the crew have had three sheep, but the great number of Ruskallah's cigars have been divided among the cook, waiter, crew, sheikhs, and consuls generally.

Tuesday, 16th.

We are in sight of Cairo, and even at this distance the citadel towers up superbly. Mingled with the real satisfaction with which we look back on our voyage as singularly fortunate in relation to health, weather, and accidents, there is the inevitable regret which accompanies the termination of all pleasant things. All partings have their serious side, but when we dismiss, probably for ever, a mode of life so unique as this, that seriousness becomes sorrow. We have felt in our little world so sheltered from the storms that rage without in the world beyond it,— we have so grown, as it were, into the Nile,

STREET FIGURES.

its climate, and its pleasures, that we feel
a little as did that prisoner of the Bastile
who could not bear the weight of his
recovered liberty.

Not that this journey up the Nile is a
talisman for every temperament and all
conditions. Health is of course essential
to enjoy it, and occupation is as needful as
health, and that occupation should be
drawn from this river-life. Studies, the
gravest and the most thoughtful, can best
be enjoyed in the presence of the objects
which stimulate and explain them, and the
daily recurrence of lovely effects in sky
and water, and the invitation the crumbling
glories of old extend on every side, tempt
the sketcher with what will task the most
delicate pencil.

The exhausted man of business (though
the repose of these scenes will give him
new strength for endeavour) will often
suffer from ennui, if his thought is here
but still haunting the paths he has
abandoned ; and the man who neither reads

nor sketches may be certain to find some
weary hours.   For him the gun is indeed
a boon, and his little excursions for the
abundant game will tone and brace him
for the quiet which neither art nor literature enriches.

Besides finding a little library of its own
in our dahabeah, and piles of little volumes
which we owe to the enterprise of Baron
Tauchnitz, the books which we have found
most useful, and which have most instructed
us are the works of Lepsius, Sharpe, and
Mariette Bey.   Wilkinson and Lane are
deservedly indispensable to all, and we
have found these authors so thorough and
compact with learning that we are hourly
almost refreshing ourselves by returning to
them.

Of books of travel, the brave and
speculative Miss Martineau, the graceful
and glowing pages of George William
Curtis, the modest yet accurate observation
of Stevens, the exceptional and useful
suggestions found in the " Nile without a

Dragoman," the pleasant touches to be found in the "Attractions of the Nile," and last, not least, the incredible adventures and pathos of our great humourist—from these all we have drawn instruction and delight.

But there are two other books which should, as it were, be melted into the mind of the traveller, the one for the truth and poetry, through which we see Eastern life as through some coloured and glowing medium, and the other for the reverential interest which it breathes around the paths of prophets and saints of old—the Arabian Nights and the Bible are alone.

Herodotus is the only classic the traveller is likely to find accessible. Diodorus Siculus, Manetho, Plutarch, and the early Alexandrian writers, he will be likely to find quoted here and there in the authors we have above named. But Herodotus, garrulous and trustful as a child, and, like a child, with unexplained and mysterious reticences, is possessed by almost every dahabeah. Though his book does not treat very largely of Egypt, there are a thousand stories of Greek and Persian in it, of which one will never weary, and in the sublime struggle at Thermopylae, to which we owe the Europe we possess, one will find a needful offset to the stupendous claims of Egypt, as a make-weight for the northern shores of the Mediterranean.

The Nile, feeling perhaps that it has indulged us too much, seems to wish to take leave of us with a fillip.

For three days we have been in what we must call a storm——the wind blowing a gale, and whole nights of rain. Even when the wind has favoured us, it has been so severe we have been obliged to tie up. But in compensation we have run off forty miles in a few hours. The injury to the smaller craft on the river has been great. We have seen damaged cargoes drying upon the bank, and the mournful crews of five wrecks waiting there for better days.

An English dahabeah was driven

aground for several hours, and we saw an American boat in trouble, apparently from a broken main-yard.

Two nights since, Ruskallah, in spite of the rain, went for a couple of hours to the hills for jackals. Though he got none, later in the night two jackals ventured very near the boat, as our sailors noticed. Our chickens (which they love) at night are always in coops, and the boat which contains the sheep is kept at night on our river-side.

We saw a large fox trotting along the opposite bank, profiting by the tumult of the storm, as if he were master of the situation. We have an additional gazelle. Our little beauty was named " Kom Ombos," from the place at which it was procured, and for the same reason this older one we christened " Minieh." Our little dove grows and improves daily. Our playful Kiki has attained the dignity of matronhood, apparently without knowing it. We have but to lament the loss of our baby crocodile.

Though now slavery is illegal in Egypt, yet slaves are secretly brought to Cairo and sold. To-day we passed two dahabeahs laden with that merchandise. Though it was secreted, we got a glimpse of a face at the window of one boat, and knew that its cargo was Abyssinian girls.

Our little slave Aboo Simbel looked wistfully at these boats, rejoicing to know what he had escaped. When told that there were plenty more boys like himself where he came from, he exclaimed : " Bring them all down here!" Though still weak from what he has suffered, he learns every day to do something useful. His dejected face now brightens with a laugh, and he is at home in his coat and trousers. But with all his good will, it will take time to fashion his awkward hands, to stimulate his fallow brain, as beseems so willing a lad.

In taking leave of the Nile, it is pleasant to think that our voyage, so delightful to ourselves, has added one freeman for the world's service, who, so far as he can, will share in what we enjoy.

The Pyramids of Saccarah are in full sight, and this will be probably our last night on the Nile. We have still two days before us ere our allotted term of ninety days is accomplished.

A visit to the tombs at Saccarah nobly completed our journey. They express in their intention perhaps the highest reach of old Egyptian thought, and worthy of fellowship with the pure ideal of Christianity.

Mariette Bey, a modern Frenchman, and probably no fanatic, simply says that these tombs consecrate the paternal affection of the Deity, who took upon himself the humble form of the ox, the animal nearest to man, and the most useful to him. These disguised Gods are indeed royally lodged in their palaces of death. No earthly king now procures such burial. As we, penetrating the darkness, and

descending an inclined plane, came upon
these vast sarcophagi, each one holding
the sacred bull or ox, we felt the sentiment
of grandeur they inspired.

They are nearly a dozen of them, each
a solid rock of polished granite, and some
of their huge lids awry, as if the Romans
who so disturbed them, in the hope of
finding something within of value, had
been gone but an instant. This confusion
of epochs is one of the chief charms and
wonders of Egypt. The prone and half-
buried obelisk near Assouan betrays tool
marks, as if the swarthy workman might
return to-morrow, and at Kom Ombos,
and many another temple, the unfinished
outline of the sculptor, makes us his
breathless contemporary.

And certainly, the fact is that the older
the work, the more venerable the temple,
the nearer it comes to us. All supreme
excellence is ever young and of the day of
the beholder. That which is maimed, in-
complete, whose beauty is false or debased,

gets at once removed to the far limit of death and disgrace, even though its date be our own. No such antiquity as fashions of fifty or a hundred years ago if true taste did not keep them for us ever young. And yet how a line of Homer or Shakspeare, an outline of Phidias, seems not only contemporaneous with us, but ready for farther flight abreast of all the future centuries.

And no satisfactory explanation do we yet have of this marvellous perfection of art and architecture at what we used to call the Dawn of Creation. How comes it, if the new theory be true of man's painful and slow emergence from barbarism and bestial conditions—how comes it that the temple at Abydus has the secure beauty of perfection ?

There is nothing feeble or tentative in its sculptured figures ; they move like the thoughts of the poet, serene and buoyant in the sunny present, and ask no allowance for immaturity or incompleteness.

The best explanation of such a marvel would seem to be in the idea of the flower-like growth to perfection of certain races and certain blooms of thought.

The movement is upward till all that hinders or encumbers the overshadowing ideal falls off, leaving the blossom of beauty for ever young and immortal. Then comes the withdrawal of the life force, the debased or dead repetition of a form whence the joyous youth has departed. The lovely blossom hardens into stone and formula. The spirit eludes and flies elsewhere, while the prostrate worshippers but surround a lifeless shell.

And in proportion to the splendour of the former life is the vacuity of the present death. The sublime and spiritual conceptions of earliest Egypt but stood for a vulgar idolatry in a later day.

But man's apprehension cannot be mistaken as to the high meaning of these Egyptian temples. Not to enclose or consecrate as idols the perishing life of common animals were reared these shrines.

They speak to our spirit, and we do not misunderstand them. It is no chance, no illusory nobleness which they breathe. Deep calleth unto deep. Our natures are searched by the· powerful glance of those faces, and it is not till we, unquestioning, surrender to their meaning that we know the height and the depth to which they carry us.

That serenity of sweetness, that sunshine of faith in which these old figures move, we have known before.

Whenever the spirit can find the calm in which the good and only Father mirrors himself, in hours of stillness and happy trust, we regain it. It shines for us in the manly face of the Theseus of Phidias, and the wave still whispers of it which breaks upon the shore of the sea of Homer. It is man when his thought is perfected—when his work is at one with Nature and some unbeheld ideal—then our race anticipates

x

its longing, and produces masterpieces with which Time has nothing to do, and which, smiling in immortal Youth, continue to instruct and charm all succeeding generations.

We were at our last stopping place on the Nile by four o'clock in the afternoon, and had abundant time to prepare for the *table d'hôte* at Shepheards.

On the cheerful terrace before the house we found many companions of our voyage.

And there, too, in front, were the same ebullient swarms of donkey-boys and runners we had left. They received us with Arabian explosions of welcome. And there, too, was the wistful and melancholy face of the snake-charmer and juggler; and he cried as before when he saw us "too clever," and offered to dip into his capacious bag of wonders.

I noticed that over the way the French house had soared a story while we were away, and by so much blotting out the

enchanting Cairo of old and for it substi-
tuting the Paris with which Mr. Hauseman
has familiarised us.

We sighed to think of so much romance
departing, and we also sighed to know that
the Nile might never more glide through
our lives, and that its book of magic delights
was for us closed for ever.

THE END.

Printed by R. & R. CLARK, *Edinburgh.*

Check Out More Titles From HardPress Classics Series In this collection we are offering thousands of classic and hard to find books. This series spans a vast array of subjects – so you are bound to find something of interest to enjoy reading and learning about.

Subjects:
Architecture
Art
Biography & Autobiography
Body, Mind &Spirit
Children & Young Adult
Dramas
Education
Fiction
History
Language Arts & Disciplines
Law
Literary Collections
Music
Poetry
Psychology
Science
…and many more.

Visit us at www.hardpress.net

CPSIA information can be obtained
at www.ICGtesting.com
Printed in the USA
BVHW041443140819
555860BV00026B/2228/P

9 780461 014228